# FRISBEE <sub>disc</sub> Sports and Games

LIBRARY
COLLEGE OF ST. BENEDICT
St. Joseph, Minnesota 56374

# FRISBEE disc
# Sports and Games

Charles Tips

Dan Roddick

Photographs by Mike Fluitt
Drawings by Byron Sewell
Diagrams by Larry Gonick

CELESTIAL ARTS
Millbrae, California

Copyright © 1979 by Charles Tips
Celestial Arts
231 Adrian Road, Millbrae, California 94030

No part of this book may be reproduced by any mechanical, photographic, or electronic process, or in the form of a phonographic recording, nor may it be stored in a retrieval system, transmitted, or otherwise copied for public or private use without the written permission of the publisher.

First printing: March 1979
Made in the United States of America

**Library of Congress Cataloging in Publication Data**

Tips, Charles, 1949-
    Frisbee, sports and games.

    Includes index.
    1. Flying discs (Game)    I. Roddick, Dan, 1948- joint author.    II. Title.
GV1097.F7T57    796.2    78-67849
ISBN 0-89087-233-3

The use of the trademark FRISBEE and other trademarks using the word FRISBEE in this book is with the permission of and under license from Wham-O Mfg. Co., 835 E. El Monte St., San Gabriel, California. FRISBEE is a registered trademark of Wham-O Mfg. Co., U.S. Trademark Reg. No. 679,186 issued, May 26, 1959, for toy flying saucers for toss games. References in the title and text of this book to FRISBEE and FRISBEE discs and saucers are intended to be and are limited solely to the disc products manufactured and sold by Wham-O Mfg. Co. under the trademarks FRISBEE, SUPER PRO FRISBEE, MINI FRISBEE, FASTBACK FRISBEE, PRO MODEL FRISBEE. Use of the term FRISBEE without the generic term "disc" is made only for historical accuracy.

Use of the official rules of the games with permission of and through the courtesy of the International Frisbee disc Association.

Use of the official rules of Ultimate with permission of Irv Kalb.

1 2 3 4 5 6 7 8 — 84 83 82 81 80 79

For Jared, Shayna, Jon Travis, Tyler, J. J., and the future of disc play

But the moment finally comes in every culture when the larger world itself begins to change in ways that confound the old games and the old rules.

—George Leonard

When a ball dreams, it dreams it's a Frisbee.

—Stancil Johnson

# Contents

Introduction  9

1. Field Events  15
2. Self-Caught Flights  28
3. Double Disc Court  34
4. Golf  42
5. Freestyle  52
6. Guts  76
7. Ultimate  89

Appendix I Other Disc Games  106

Appendix II Records  111

Glossary  113

Acknowledgments  119

Key to Photograph Identification  120

All photos Mike Fluitt except: **Sam Barron**–10, 23, 26, 27, 29 (l, r, & bottom), 32, 51 (l), 55 (r), 57 (r), 59 (top), 60 (l, top & bottom), 63 (top), 64, 66 (l, top & bottom), 67 (bottom & top r), 68 (top), 70 (bottom 1), 71 (bottom), 73 (top r), 85 (l), 87 (r), 92 (l), 93 (r), 96, 97 (bottom); **Betsy Gilbert**–1, 5; **David Shelton**–18; **Ken Van Sickle**–43 (bottom); **Donnell Tate**–72-73; **Larry Horowitz**–74 (top), 75 (top); **Matt Ryman**–74 (bottom); **Dan Poynter**–75 (bottom); **Linda Agress**–85 (r); **Louann Rank**–97 (top); **Larry LaSota**–108. Cover photo by Sam Barron

# Introduction

Sport has gone crazy in our generation, since Sputnik launched the Space Age. Football, baseball, and basketball enjoy more popularity than ever, but they are giving ground to a flood of other athletic activities. Soccer and hockey are joining the ranks of major sports in this country. People are bicycling, running, swimming, bowling, climbing, rafting in incredible numbers. Amid this enthusiasm for sport spring the seedlings of a new order of sports, namely, hang gliding, skateboarding, and disc play. They embody the Space Age—flight, freedom, exploration and ephemeral control.

Frisbee disc play is a modern phenomenon. Eighty million people have tried it. More discs are sold each year than baseballs, basketballs and footballs combined. But the exact origins of disc play remain pleasantly and tantalizingly shrouded in uncertainty. There is evidence of considerable fascination with saucerlike objects prior to the commercial production of plastic discs. Paper plates, records, pie tins, and can tops all spent some time in the sky. Their appeal was obvious—they truly flew. Pie tins get most of the credit for pre-plastic play, probably because they perform fairly well. Some tins fly well even by today's standards.

Despite this early activity, there was no real precedent for the flying disc. It fell into our hands without instructions. Fortunately, its entrancing flight was enough to keep people exploring the potential of this new plaything. Enthusiasts were faced with a unique opportunity to develop play as they saw fit. And the creative possiblities soon proved to be the disc's best feature.

People don't invent new games with baseballs or footballs; they play what they're "supposed" to play. Try a behind-the-back-swings-only game of tennis at a country club and people will be incensed that you don't "play right." And so the flying disc became a magnet for maverick sports talents who preferred following their own inclinations to structured play. The fusion of this talent with the disc's natural potential made for an incredible rush of creative activity.

You may wonder why we are dwelling on the invention of games before we've even presented a single one. The answer is that the invention of a new game is an important step in an ongoing process of discovery. It is a learning experience for the inventor, and something that can be shared with others. Furthermore, we want you to understand how the games in this book came about, so that you will be better able to alter them to your particular needs of ability, location, etc. Mainly, the invention of games has been an integral part of Frisbee disc play for so long that it's in our blood.

This book and its predecessor, *Frisbee by the Masters,* record the progress of the creativity that has led to present-day playing techniques and games. Perhaps the most important information you can gain from either book is that the potential for further discovery remains in abundance. More games? Let's have 'em. New catches? Entirely possible. And you could be the originator. These pages cover what has been done, and try to shed some light on what may come—what *will* come is in your head.

## DEVELOPING DISC GAMES

Two avenues are open for developing games with a flying disc. A game can be formulated by analogy to an established game, or it can evolve as the outgrowth of an enjoyable activity.

Basebee is a nice example of an analogy game. People pick up the concept readily because they know baseball's rules, and most of the disc rules are obvious:

• The flinger throws to the baseman who must try to catch anything within reach (pivot foot on home plate).

The most popular Frisbee disc playing models. Clockwise from left: Pro model, World Class 141-G ("G" stands for "grams"), Premium Fastback, World Class 165-G, Super Pro, World Class 97-G, World Class 119-G. Center: Mini disc.

- Three misses and baseman is out; four throws out of reach and baseman walks.
- Flies, bunts, and grounders are played as in baseball.
- Baseman must throw immediately after catching the pitch.
- Runners may be put out by being hit with the disc below the knees when off base.

Variations such as one- or two-handed catching, trick catching, or Guts-speed pitching make Basebee adaptable to a wide range of abilities.

Conversions to football, hockey, tennis, or any other sport are just as easy. Refining the rules to meet the needs of your group is part of the fun. It also gives perspective on the concept of rules in general.

There are several obvious limitations to the disc when it comes to imitating other games. It does not bounce for dribbling, and it is not easy to propel with an implement, to name two. The challenge is in coming up with alternatives. Airbrushing, for instance, makes an exciting alternative to dribbling.

Probably everyone who has ever played with a disc for any length of time has devised challenges to suit particular locations: a hallway ("Let's see who can throw to the end without hitting the walls"), an arbor ("One point for every tree you pass"), a planter box ("Two points if you hit it, five if you land in it").

These games crop up wherever there are disc players and a place to play. For instance, every group of lifeguards has a game centering on the need to throw accurately and avoid getting wet. One club has designed a game to be played on a gigantic three-tiered fountain. Such games are special because they are perfect for those people, at that place, at that time. They may last only a few minutes, or they may develop into popular sports.

There are a number of general considerations in designing games and ensuring wide popularity for them:

- Keep it simple.
- Avoid outlawing undesirable activities, such as very hard throws. Instead, design the rules to make activities that don't fit the game concept unproductive.
- Resist using special equipment.

- Look for balance between offense and defense.
- Attempt to accommodate as wide a range of abilities as possible.
- Consider the game's appeal for both player and spectator.
- Make use of the disc's distinctive properties of flight.

Again, you can also make up disc games by simply modifying the games in this book to suit your interests. Don't let the OFFICIAL RULES daunt you. The gods of play smile on those who take whatever measures necessary to enjoy themselves.

RULES AND OFFICIALS

Disc games have traditionally been played without officials, even for national and world championship titles. The duty to play within the rules rests on the players themselves.

Sometimes, observers are used to aid in difficult perceptual situations. For example, it is very difficult for the opposing players to call a double disc situation in Double Disc Court. Ultimate, too, sometimes uses observers, but they are rarely called upon. In disc sports the players' responsibility is playing for the best interest of the team within the restrictions of the rules, not trying to get away with anything they can when the official is not looking.

Many people consider Frisbee disc play noncompetitive. Essentially, that is true, but several disc sports are competitive, even aggressive. Nevertheless, disc games have traditionally been played without officials, even for national and world championship titles.

This has been possible because the players have adopted an informal code: The duty to play within the rules rests on the players themselves. Ultimate

raises this code to a formal statement in the rules, and we comment on that in chapter 7.

Sometimes, observers are used to aid in difficult perceptual situations; for example, it is often impossible for any of the players to call a double disc situation in Double Disc Court. Ultimate, too, sometimes uses observers, but they are seldom called on. Observers are consulted when the players question a play; they do not make calls otherwise.

So far, the decision not to use officials has worked well. While the use of officials could have prevented several hundred arguments, the arguments are actually a healthy thing. Arguments don't get heated; when it becomes obvious both sides feel strongly, a compromise is sought, such as taking the play in question over.

First-time viewers often remark, "That's fine if you don't want to use referees now, but you'll need them when the big bucks come in." Perhaps, but it would be a shame to see game officials become a reality simply from the accumulated weight of many such cynical expectations. Players already play for respect and the honor of highly valued titles. Their desire to win is extremely high. Can money change things so much?

The answer will be "no" if players continue to encourage each other to play by the rules. In some sports, athletes receive subtle encouragement to try to get away with rule violations. This will not be the case in disc sports as long as we are all willing to set the necessary examples.

## ORGANIZATION

The International Frisbee disc Association (IFA) was formed in 1967 and now has more than 110,000 members worldwide. The two most visible functions of the IFA are publication of *Frisbee disc World* magazine and organization of the North American Tournament Series. The North American Tournament Series, or National Championship Series as it is also known, comprises more than twenty disc-sport meets held each year from March to August in cities across Canada and the United States. Points are earned in these meets toward an invitation to participate in the World Frisbee disc Championship (WFC) held in the Rose Bowl in Pasadena, California, on the last weekend of August each year.

*Frisbee disc World* reports the schedules of these tournaments and the results. There is also news of state and local meets, new records set, games and techniques, club activities, and other information of interest to the enthusiast.

The IFA has left most of the responsibility for the direction disc sports will take in the hands of the affiliate clubs and has acted instead as a communication center to help promote such interest. Affiliate clubs are the local clubs around the world. They range in organization from small groups of friends who get together occasionally to play to widespread programs covering entire states or regions, with their own newsletters, meets, and regular activities.

## LIFETIME SPORT

These games can be with you for life if you like. Once you tire of the strain of Guts or lose your stamina for Ultimate, there's always golf. Freestyle can be enjoyed at any pace. Feel like a sociable backyard game? Try Double Disc Court.

Disc sports are unique in providing so much with a set of basic skills. Not only can you play at whatever pace you like, you have a choice of game from every type of sport interaction. For team play there's Ultimate. One-to-one and doubles competition is found in Double Disc Court. To get aggressive, try Guts. If you want no competition, only to collaborate with a partner, there's freestyle. If you just want to go out and try to knock a few points off your score, there's golf. The skills of any one of these transfer readily to any other. And if these aren't enough outlets for you, you can always invent a game of your own.

This book is intended to complement *Frisbee by the Masters*. Each is self-contained; that is, you don't need one to understand the other. But, of course, the techniques of play described in *Frisbee by the Masters* are what these games are built on; in those places where information in the earlier book is particularly pertinent, we have provided a page reference.

We should point out that the terminology used for describing spin has changed since *Frisbee by the Masters* came out. "Clock spin," which was referred to as "left spin," pertains to a right-hander's backhand and a left-hander's sidearm or wrist flip. "Counter spin" is the term that replaces "right spin." We hope you will find these terms clearer.

# 1. Field Events

The urge to test the limits of one's ability provided the force behind the first departures from the toss format of play. Youngsters playing with the early Pluto Platters asked themselves naturally enough, "How far can I throw this thing?" "Is this as accurate as a ball?" Questions such as "How far can I throw this thing straight up?" never jelled into a common activity, but they did provide information of a sort about the dimensions of this new plaything.

Each experiment gave new feedback about the player's ability and the properties of the disc. The experiments grew more demanding: "What happens if I throw it out this way at a steeper angle?" Almost all Frisbee disc events are outgrowths of this self-testing urge. Guts grew from the desire to see how fast the disc could be thrown and the resulting desire to see if such throws could be caught. Golf grew from the desire to see if certain objects in the field of play could be hit at long range. Not until many of these questions had been answered and become ingrained as player skill could play proceed to the level of creating games by adapting them from other

Charging the line. The run-up serves two purposes: to get the thrower into the "groove" and to give the muscles a good stretch just before release.

sources, as is the case with Ultimate and Double Disc Court.

So, when we talk about the field events—Distance, Accuracy, Maximum Time Aloft, and Throw, Run & Catch—we are talking about the basic relationship of player to disc. We are talking about the fundamental questions: "How far?" "How accurate?" "How long?" This chapter will deal with Distance and Accuracy. Maximum Time Aloft (MTA) and Throw, Run & Catch (TRC) are covered in the next chapter.

## DISTANCE

While there must have been many thousands of distance throwing attempts in schoolyards and playgrounds around the country, it is easy to pinpoint the origin of modern interest in the event. When Jay Shelton and Steve Sewell moved to Berkeley, California, in the late '60s, their pursuit of knowledge of the disc was almost a passion. Soon talented players joined them: Bob May, Victor Malafronte, Roger Barrett, Steve Gottlieb, and Chuck Pitt. The first formal distance competitions were held on the Cal campus between the Berkeley Frisbee Group and the Stanford players during Big Game Week. The winner was determined by who hit highest up on a building across the plaza on which the event was staged.

By 1970, the hundred-yard barrier had been broken by Bob May throwing backhand and Victor Malafronte throwing sidearm. Interestingly, the disc that broke the barrier was concocted by Victor from a Pluto Platter wedged into a shaved-down Pro Model rim.

**World distance record holder, John Kirkland, is unsurpassed in his ability to get full body rotation. Notice that between the fourth and sixth photos his shoulders and head have turned through more than 180 degrees.**

The International Frisbee Tournament became the showcase for distance throwing prowess from 1970 to 1974. However, measurement procedures at IFT were inaccurate at best, biased at worst. The field was almost always downhill, and "measurement" consisted of someone looking through a surveyor's transit and making an estimate.

The important thing is that the IFT sparked competitive desire. By 1973, the East had players who could challenge the Berkeley players' domination of the event. John Connelly won IFT that year with a mark of 309 feet. John Kirkland and Dave Johnson of Boston dominated distance throwing for the next several years. Dave broke the 400-foot barrier in 1976. John holds the current official world record at 444 feet with a backhand throw. Mike Conger of Maryland is the other member of the "400 club."

Three players have achieved marks over 500 feet on unofficial throws, two with sidearms: Victor Malafronte, Dave Johnson, and Ken Westerfield are the members of the "500 club."

## TECHNIQUE

Throwing a disc for distance provides more challenge than discus, javelin, or shotput. The lightness of the disc makes control particularly demanding. That the disc actually flies makes the trajectory of flight especially critical. Wind is a major factor. And the throwing motions for disc distance are just as complex as those of discus and shotput.

There is an excellent discussion of distance technique in chapter 9 of *Frisbee by the Masters,* and those who wish to learn more about this event are encouraged to look there. The present discussion will be limited to the basic components of technique and the factors that most influence good performance.

*Wind.* The first factor the distance thrower must analyze is nature's gift to Frisbee disc play—the breeze. It irks top players to hear someone comment, "Yeah, but he had the wind at his back," because they know that playing the wind incorrectly produces little help. Finding the exact point at which the wind will give you the most assistance is a fine art that requires extensive probing of the downfield space with practice tosses. Furthermore, a given faster wind many not be as helpful as another slower wind, depending on features of the field and climatic conditions. Expect to spend a long time learning the nuances of the wind.

*Grip.* Any slippage in the grip subtracts directly from the force applied to the disc. Maintain a firm grip. The Berkeley power grip is the choice in backhands (see FBTM, p. 84). The forefinger curls around the rim and the other fingers pull snugly on the cheek. The thumb lies far forward on the topside of the disc. The Bonopane grip constitutes the only currently popular variation. The index finger rests on top of the thumb. This odd position provides for a low-resistance, negative-angle release.

The sidearm grip finds the first two fingers wedged against the cheek of the disc and the thumb on top (see FBTM, p. 92). The middle finger, which does most of the work, should be bent slightly so that it presses into the cheek rather than simply lie along it.

*Run-up.* Athletic movement is improved when the muscles involved are stretched immediately prior to performance. That, and finding your "groove" are the purpose of a run-up. Any advantage gained by stretching can be more than offset if the run-up does not blend into the delivery motion. The complex motions of delivery must be learned with a slow, deliberate walk-up. Only after they are down pat can faster and faster run-ups be attempted.

**Jay Shelton demonstrates his late-'60s distance technique.**

# Field Events

*Foot Plant.* Some players are of the opinion that a leaping, pirouetting delivery will ultimately produce the greatest results because of greater centripetal force. Not only is the force not greater, but absence of a foot plant prevents energy in the lower body from being transferred up to assist the throw. Any slippage during the foot plant subtracts directly from the force applied to the disc, just as with grip slippage.

The sidearm foot plant is somewhat more complex than its backhand counterpart. The rear foot plants first and is used to drive the hips forward until the forward foot plants and the rear leg swings around to add momentum to the rotation of the body. In the backhand, the forward foot is the only plant.

**A backhand distance throw (left, top to bottom). 1. The right foot plants. 2. The hips and back initiate rotation. The upper arm is thrown forward. 3. The hips drive forward. 4. The wrist begins cocking. 5. Release. 6. Follow-through.**

**A sidearm distance throw (right, top to bottom). 1. The right foot plants. 2. The elbow is thrown downward. 3. The hips thrust forward. 4. The left foot plants. 5. The wrist begins cocking and the forearm whips forward. 6. Release.**

*Delivery.* The idea is to get the whole body thrusting forward and rotating into the throw, increasing momentum until it threatens to topple the player over. Every fiber in the body must contribute. Only a few players, most notably John Kirkland, currently throw their head around to add to the momentum.

**The sidearm offers more potential than the backhand as a distance throw except that it is more complicated to master. Notice, for instance, how far out of line the shoulders move from the hips to produce maximum leverage.**

Some backhand throwers will even swing their rear leg *behind* their planted leg in a very counterproductive effort to maintain balance.

The biggest failing, and consequently the best area for improvement, is lack of hip displacement, particularly in backhanders. The hips should drive forward a couple of feet after the foot plant and initiate rotation at the same time. The effect on the body should be to jerk the back and torso into action. Almost all the deliveries you see, even in topflight competition, end with the hips positioned behind the planted foot. Not only is that an incredible loss of power, but it prevents most of the power in the legs from the run-up, plant, and drive from being transferred to the torso.

Field Events

**The run-up and follow-through of a sidearm delivery.**

## TRAINING

Mastering the mechanics of delivery is the big hurdle. For beginning backhands, the "X" position yields good results quickly: Stand with your heels on the desired target line. Grip the disc with both hands, one on each side. Move the front foot a little forward and shift the disc forward at the same time. Cross the rear leg behind the front as you swing the disc well back (feel the stretch?) Bring the front leg forward a whole stride, and, as you feel the next stretch, let the disc fly, dropping the grip of the rear hand at the top of the forward motion.

As you get more comfortable with this drill, try pushing more with your rear leg, try rotating your head with the delivery, and, finally, try incorporating a longer walk-up and then run-up.

When you are throwing correctly, you'll feel it—from the rush of blood into your fingertips to the dizzying sensation of almost flying off your feet.

*Flight.* The key is to get the disc up with its nose down. This produces the effect Stancil Johnson refers to as "nose gliding." There is not much margin for a good throw—slightly too low and the disc gets no carry from the breeze; a little too high and the flight sags and drifts. Getting a high/negative-attack combination is tricky but essential. To begin, throw slight roll curves fairly high. They are not ideal, but they will allow you to observe nose gliding.

**The "X" position is ideal for beginning distance throwers. It offers a good stretch and wind-up without all the complications of a run-up.**

There are several things you should do to help condition yourself for distance throwing (and this goes for MTA, TRC, Guts, and other events). Perhaps most important is to stretch and strengthen the muscles of the back, chest, and shoulders. Slow, yoga-type stretching exercises are best. Workouts with light weights (around ten pounds) will strengthen the arms.

The throwing motion can be strengthened by going through the motions with a one- or two-pound weight. If you can fashion a disc-shaped weight, so much the better. You might also try rigging up a spring or elastic band to pull as you go through your throwing motion.

After every distance throw, you will want to ask yourself the following five questions:

1. Was I aware of the wind?
2. Did my run-up blend into the delivery?
3. Did I stretch my muscles well prior to delivery?
4. Did my muscles move in correct sequence—torso, then leg, then arm?
5. Did I get maximum leverage from my hips, shoulder, and arm?

Of course, you will also want to notice how far each of your throws travels.

## DISC SELECTION

Choosing a good stock of distance discs is a pragmatic process. Simply throw twenty or so candidates and pick them up. The longer flights deserve additional testing, assuming your deliveries were uniform. Discs vary greatly even within a given model and mold. Evaluate each disc individually.

All the discs in your stock should have the same flight characteristics. You want your distance throw grooved, and you cannot, therefore, be making adjustments for each disc from one throw to the next. This will almost always mean that all your discs will be from the same mold. Most players go with the 40 mold 119-G model.

Weighing the discs might help your prediction ability. Heavier discs of a given model are usually more stable and will travel farther.

## FUTURE

Many times the cry has gone up for some sort of limit on allowable wind velocities, but the disc is so profoundly affected by the wind it's just not that simple. Indoor distance throwing is a surer test of raw ability, but then playing the wind is a fine art. It is possible that a perfect performance in less than ideal conditions will not yield as good a mark as a lesser performance in ideal conditions. But optimum wind conditions occur frequently enough that the records of distance, MTA, and the other wind-influenced events reflect the state of the art accurately. Sooner or later, everybody gets a chance under ideal conditions. If they blow it, well, that's the breaks.

Look for the outdoor mark to zoom over 600 feet and the indoor mark over 300 feet soon. Improvements in technique and discs (and there is plenty of room in both areas) will assure this.

It is curious that only a couple of players have availed themselves of local track-and-field coaches for advice on their technique. Those players who have sought such instruction have benefited. Good coaching could have tremendous impact on the disc field events.

## RELATED GAMES

The distance event has seen many variations in its time. Vertical distance is gauged by how far you can hit up the side of a tall wall. Downhill distance is always popular and has slightly different throwing strategies because of the difference in wind flow. Circular distance is thrown in any direction so that there is no out of bounds and so that changes in wind direction can be quickly accommodated.

Accuracy distance is held often, particularly in juniors' competitions. The idea is to throw downfield along a line and have the disc land as close to the line as possible. Net distance is measured as the distance downfield minus the distance away from the line.

Medley distance has been tried on occasion and probably deserves more attention. The idea is to accumulate distance from each of several different types of deliveries. A competitor's distance might be the total of, say, a roller, a behind-the-back throw, a push throw, a wrist flip, a hook thumber, and a butterfly. Such an event would encourage serious inquiry into the potential of throws other than the backhand and sidearm.

## ACCURACY

The roots of accuracy go back to early golflike games. In the strict sense, accuracy events are standardized and the results may be compared, making

**The underhand delivery is sometimes seen in Accuracy competition. The position of the retriever and the field judge are shown here.**

# DISTANCE

## GROUND RULES

All throws must be delivered from behind the 15-foot foul line (any part of body on line or on ground over line before or during the release constitutes a foul). Competitor may cross line after release.

Each player must deliver his four throws within two minutes of being called. Unattempted trials are recorded as fouls. The head judge will call "time-warning—30 seconds" at 1:30 of the throwing period.

Any throw landing completely outside of the out-of-bounds lines counts as a foul. Should a throw strike any fixed object while in flight outside the sector it is scored as an automatic zero. Any flight touched by a spectator, dog, etc. while in flight over the sector must be taken over. Neither the thrower nor the scorekeeper may decide otherwise. Players should have a disc for each attempt when they are called to throw.

## CONTEST PROCEDURE

First Round–all competitors receive four attempts (cut to 15).

Second Round–15 competitors receive four attempts (place 30th to 6th and cut to 5 finalists based on single best mark in second round).

Finals–finalists receive four attempts (place first to fifth on single best mark of finals).

Ties for first place should be broken by giving the tied competitors an additional set of attempts. The better mark in that set determines the winner.

In Indoor Distance, winner may be based on single best effort in any round due to constancy of conditions.

## FIELD LAYOUT

A–Measuring point, center of foul line
B–Stakes topped with streamers and labeled 100, 200, 300, 400. Out-of-bounds lines include a range of 70 degrees and should be visibly marked.

Field should be set to throw with the prevailing wind. Unblocked air flow from behind foul line is most desirable. Field must be essentially level for record consideration.

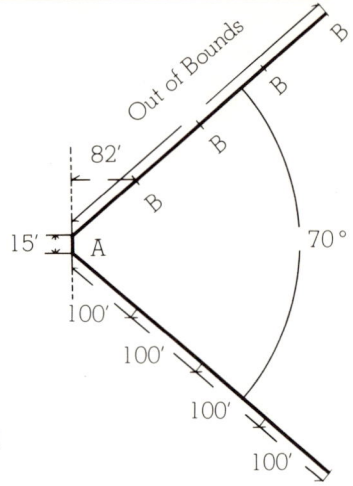

## MEASUREMENT

All throws should be measured from center of the foul line (A) to the center of the disc where it first strikes the ground. Distances should be registered to the nearest 6 inches.

A 300-foot tape should lie in the throwing area for use after each set of throws. Each attempt should be marked with the disc thrown and the best of each competitor's attempts should be measured immediately following the set of throws. A one-hundred foot tape should be held by the measuring crew for marks over 300 feet.

## STAFFING

Head Judge–calls competitors and calls time warnings.

Measurement Crew (4 persons)
Person No. 1–Records and announces competitor's throws, marks throws.
Person No. 2–Holds tape at measuring point A.
Persons No. 3 & 4–Aid in marking throws.

# ACCURACY

## FORMAT

Competitor receives four attempts from each throwing line. Any order of attempts is permissible. Total hits (Frisbee disc passes entirely through Hoop) out of 28 total attempts constitutes competitor's score.

## CONTEST PROCEDURE

First round–cut to 15.

Second round–cut to 5 (place 15th to 6th by hits in round 2).

Finals–place first to fifth by hits in finals.

**Ties for first place should be broken by giving the tied competitors another round. The better mark in that set determines the winner.**

## STAFFING

Head Judge–calls competitors and registers hits.
Target Judge–calls out hits.
Frisbee Return Crew–one behind target, one by competitor (can be on-deck competitors).

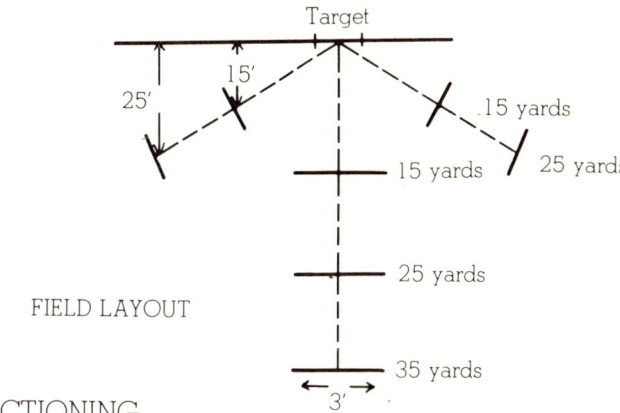

FIELD LAYOUT

## FIELD TARGET

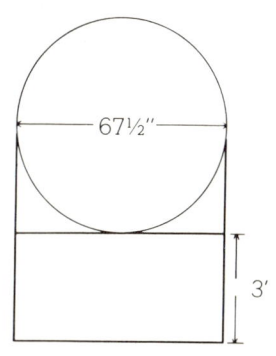

Hoop is constructed of two medium (105½" length) Hula Hoops® joined to form one hoop.

## SECTIONING

Weather change over the competitive period has always been a difficulty in Frisbee disc events. This problem has become increasingly evident as the number of entrants has risen, thus extending the length of the preliminaries. In an attempt to partially control the impact of condition variation, the sectioning procedure has been developed.

In events which may present problems of condition change, the semi-finalists should be drawn from the preliminaries in the following manner:

   1. Prior to the competition, use of sectioning procedure should be announced.

   2. The players take their preliminary attempts in the usual manner.

   3. After all players have taken their preliminary attempts, the chronological order should be divided into thirds.

   4. The top five performances from each third move on to the semi-finals.

   This technique is suggested for MTA, TRC, Distance and Accuracy competitons.

them quite different from the sort of accuracy required in golf.

Early accuracy events were poorly conceived. Targets were too small and players received too few throws. In the early IFT's for example, an automobile tire was the target and players took three tries each from forty-five yards. Three players each managed a hit in the preliminary round of the 1973 IFT, and the finals went on for thirty minutes before another hit was made.

The 1969 Pennsylvania State Championships featured Accuracy with thirty attempts at a suspended Hula Hoop from six sites arranged from 15 to 120 feet. In the same year, the Berkeley Big Game Tournament introduced Medley Accuracy, which tested a ten-throw series of skips, curves, and straight flights.

Curving shots were not required in major competition before 1975. The World Frisbee disc Championships that year featured a bizarre four-opening target made of Hula Hoops tied together, one facing forward, one on either side, and one on top. Players threw at each hoop from each of three sites. The current format was introduced by the IFA in 1976, and certification of world records began.

### TECHNIQUE

Success in Accuracy demands appropriate and immediate adjustment for observed errors. The temptation to overadjust gets even the best of play-

**The loneliness of the long-distance Accuracy thrower.**

ers. This presumes a delivery grooved well enough that it can be knowledgably and effectively altered to cope with high or uneven winds, and to make allowances for shots that miss the mark.

Many successful competitors visualize the intended flight of the disc. The reality of the throw that follows gives feedback to the player's visual image and that in turn to the next throw.

Backhands are most common. Sidearms work well even though they are released far from the line of vision. Upside-down sidearms, however, are released nearer to the line of vision than any other type of delivery, and they work well from the straight-away sites.

Staying with one delivery style would be best from the standpoint of a grooved throw, but different sites favor different throws. In general, the roll curves are more accurate than the skip curves. So, for instance, a backhander might find some advantage to throwing sidearm roll curves rather than backhand skip curves.

From the side stations, soft, arching flights have a better chance than straighter trajectories; that is, they do until the wind comes up. Then the players who have concentrated their practice on the curves are wiped out by the low, straight shooters. Experience is a must, as there are many subtleties of spin, speed, and attitude that can spell the difference between a disc tacking on a cross wind or being blown away.

Order of site selection has developed two different schools. One contends it is best to take the low-percentage sites first so that you can read the windflow on shots you are more likely to miss anyway. And, you can shake tension and get into your groove before reaching the more crucial high-percentage sites. The other faction maintains that bad wind or good, you seldom miss the close ones. You learn the wind, build confidence, and get warmed up for the longer ones.

Disc selection is personal. You want the flight characteristics of your discs to be uniform, obviously, and you will probably want larger discs with any wind because of their greater "presence." Wind won't always be a factor, but you don't want to change to an unfamiliar model if it does become one.

**A good curve shot will increase the chances of hitting the mark from the side stations.**

## FUTURE

Accuracy was removed as a World Championship event in the 1978 Tournament Series. Though the format provides a valid test of throwing control, the need for equipment, its relative dullness and time-consuming nature, and the difficulty of individual practice all contributed to its demise. It is still employed in state and local tournaments, but will not likely return to the National Series unless some improved format is devised.

# 2. Self-Caught Flights

The development of the two self-caught field events sheds light on the development of all disc games. Maximum Time Aloft and Throw, Run & Catch evolved from natural curiosity about the properties of the disc and the skills of the player, and soon led to formal competitive events.

Very likely, hundreds of early disc flingers tried in wonderment to see how long they could keep a throw suspended on the wind. Again, it was Jay Shelton and Steve Sewell who carried wonderment a step farther. In their undergraduate days at Harvard about 1965, they originated head-to-head competition in boomerang flight duration, that is, each released a disc on command and the last to catch his disc won.

After they arrived in Berkeley, this led to a game that involved throwing around light standards in a parking lot. All players released on command, and the last to make a catch was awarded a point, two points for a throw around the pole, and three for a throw that grazed the pole. By 1970, almost all the refinements of Maximum Time Aloft had been introduced by Sewell, Shelton, Steve Gottlieb, Roger Barrett, Victor Malafronte, and others.

It occurred to Stancil Johnson while participating in the Berkeley boomerang games that some of the throws were caught relatively farther from their origins than others. Stancil quickly conceived of a game which would incorporate that observation. The result was a contest in which participants threw from a circle and were awarded points for each of several concentric rings they crossed before catching their disc. Each player got five throws, and points were totalled for all five.

The first major use of the event came in the El Cerrito Recreation Department Tournament of 1972. Steve Gottlieb walked away with top honors after completing his five throws outside the outer (150 feet) ring, a creditable performance even by today's standards.

Not until 1973 did timing of MTA begin. Roger Barrett took the International Frisbee Tournament that year with a toss of 9.3 seconds. The ten-second barrier was broken the following year as John Kirkland set the world mark at Octad.

Measurement of TRC began about the same time. John Kirkland set a second world mark at the '74 Octad with a catch at 165 feet.

And that's the sequence of most disc games: Curiosity leads to attempt, attempt to success, success to a rudimentary game, the game to new discoveries, discoveries to progressively more complex events.

## Self-Caught Flights

**Throw**

**Run**

**Catch**

## TECHNIQUE

Similar technique is involved in MTA and TRC. Both are far from simple. In the first place, the disc must be inserted into an invisible window in the sky. It must arrive with precisely the right angle and attitude. The descent must be read correctly and a clean catch must be made.

To throw MTA, look into the wind and picture a huge nose thirty or forty feet in the air. Assuming you intend to throw a right-handed backhand, stand ten to twenty degrees to the left of the nose, relatively to the wind. To place your throw just right, you must sail it with a slight skip curve so that it hits squarely on the bulb of the nose. From there it will ride straight up to the bridge of the nose (a phenomenon known as towering) and fall off for a descent slightly further to your right.

Should you throw too low (seldom happens—the vast majority of errors comes from throwing too steeply), the disc will sail under the nose and continue on. Should you throw too high, the disc will hit at too great an angle and slide right back down. If

**The preferred grip and the preferred disc for MTA and TRC.**

## SELF-CAUGHT FLIGHT

This will be the official format for MTA and TRC in the North American Tournament Series beginning in 1979.

### CONTEST PROCEDURE

First Round—all competitors receive five MTA attempts. Players should be called in groups of three and take their attempts in rotation. (Cut to 30 on single best mark of round one.)

Second Round—all competitors receive five TRC attempts. All competitors receive five MTA attempts. TRC marks are ranked from first to thirtieth. MTA marks are ranked from first to thirtieth. Scores are assigned in inverse order (first gets 30 points, second gets 29, and so on) for each event. Scores are then added to determine standings. (Cut to five.)

Final Round—procedure in this round is identical to previous round. Winner is declared based on scoring in both MTA and TRC.

## MAXIMUM TIME ALOFT

### FIELD AREA

Should be contested on an essentially level and smooth area having at least 75 yards of running room in all directions from center. Unblocked wind flow is desirable.

### GROUND RULES

Each contestant should throw the disc into the air and attempt to catch it cleanly in one hand (no trapping against body) before it touches the ground. Time is measured from the instant of release until the instant the disc is first touched in the catching attempt.

After the throwing group is called, each player must throw within 15 seconds of his individual call or forfeit that attempt. A 5-second warning is given by the head judge.

Any flight touching a fixed object or touched by a spectator must be taken over, regardless of whether or not it was caught by the entrant. If the head judge deems that the entrant was interfered with in any way while in pursuit of the disc, he/she may award a rethrow. Rethrows should be taken in rotation, not immediately after judge's decision.

Should the disc be first touched at the same instant it first touches the ground and is ultimately caught it should be ruled a good and legal catch. If, however, the disc touches the ground an instant before being touched, it is a non-catch and is scored as a zero. This call should be made by the competitor.

### MEASUREMENT

The official time for each effort should be determined to the nearest 1/10 of a second from the readings of the three watches. The time should be the median (middle) time registered, e.g., 7.1, 7.0, 6.8 = 7.0, or 9.7, 9.7, 10.0 = 9.7.

### STAFFING

Head Judge—calls competitors, records times and determines cuts.

Measurement Crew—(3 persons)—measure attempts with stopwatches and determine official time.

# THROW, RUN & CATCH

### GROUND RULES

Should be contested on an essentially level and smooth area having at least 75 yards of running room in all directions from center. Unblocked wind flow is desirable. In the center of the field there should be a four-yard diameter foul circle.

Each contestant should throw the disc into the air and attempt to catch it cleanly in one hand (no trapping against body) before it touches the ground. Distance is measured from the nearest point on the foul circle to the point at which the disc is first touched in the catching attempt. Any length run is allowed prior to throw but release must be from within circle. No part of the body may be on the circle or on the ground outside the circle before or during the release.

After the group call, each player must throw within 15 seconds of his individual call or forfeit that attempt. A five-second warning is given by the head judge.

### MEASUREMENT

Each attempt should be measured and recorded. Readings should be made to the nearest 6 inches.

### STAFFING

Head Judge-calls competitors, records throws, determines cuts, and calls time warnings.

Measurement Crew (3 persons)
Person No. 1–Holds tape on circle.
Persons No. 2 & 3–Determine mark and read measurement.

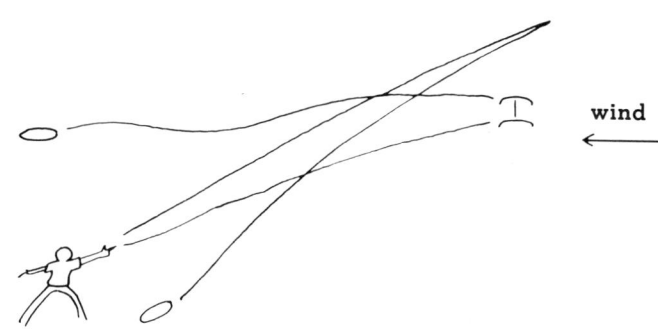

**A proper MTA throw shelfs, towers, and is carried by the wind. Throw it too steep and the disc dives back to the ground.**

you throw wide on the side straight into the wind, you might get a good MTA, but not the best possible. If you err to the side away from the wind, you are getting into TRC territory.

Depending on the disc, the wind conditions, and your throwing preference, you can also try MTA by standing to the right of the nose and sailing the disc with a slight roll curve. Either way, the disc must be made to "shelf" at the point at which it stalls against the wind, that is, it must end up level as though lying on a shelf. It would seem that a throw with greater positive attitude (with the nose up more) would present more surface area to the wind, but that matters little except in the stiffest of winds. It is the wing effect of the wind passing under and over the level disc that produces lift and the resulting tower.

If the throw has gone well to this point, the thrower can hope for "platforming," an almost level descent of the disc in the glide phase. As the disc slows, inflection points may occur. The nose comes up a bit, causing the descent to slow and adding precious tenths of seconds to the time.

Needless to say, the catch should be made as near the ground as possible. (For further discussion of MTA flights, see FBTM, p. 26.)

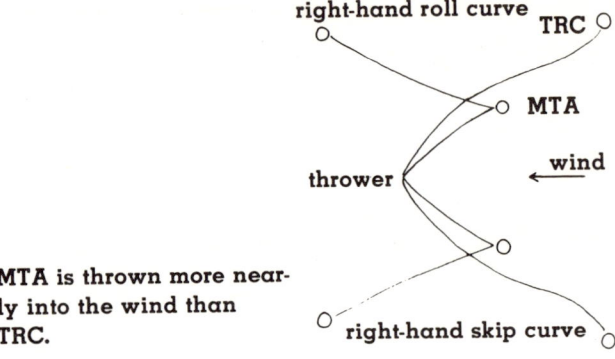

**MTA is thrown more nearly into the wind than TRC.**

**Playing the wind correctly is crucial in self-caught flight events. Dropping a few blades of grass is the standard way to test the wind, but some players use smoking incense sticks or soap bubbles to determine wind direction.**

TRC throws vary only slightly from MTA throws, but the resulting flight is very different. The TRC throw must penetrate the invisible window and continue on for distance. To accomplish this, the throw is made somewhat wider into the wind than an MTA throw, and with perhaps a little lower trajectory.

Obviously, speed of foot is important. To get the extra step, start running with the throw and read the disc on the run. You are your own target. The challenge is to throw accurately to the farthest point you can reach in the time the disc will be up. Overthrow, and there's no chance for a catch. Underthrow, and you don't reach your potential.

## DISC SELECTION

No event requires more careful selection of throwing stock than these two. Choice is like selecting fishing flies to match the spring hatch. In other words, a lot of esoteric knowledge is necessary. Top players will check mold numbers, weigh the discs to the nearest tenth of a gram, and even try to locate discs from a specific production run of a given mold. A good disc will be

- light enough to float out
- heavy enough to penetrate
- stable enough not to turn over before the shelf
- unstable enough to inflect off the tower and produce multiple inflections during the glide phase

In 1976 Tom McRann introduced the use of Wham-O's premium Fastback disc for these events. Use of Fastbacks is almost universal (particularly the FB-3 mold) because they meet the above requirements better than other disc models.

FUTURE

For some reason, the MTA record of 15 seconds has been the most durable of all disc records. Twenty seconds seems reasonable, but not one of many thousands of throws by top players has topped fifteen seconds. TRC records, on the other hand, have risen steadily in response to improvements in distance throwing and strategy. A few throws of more than one hundred yards have been narrowly missed. However, TRC was dropped from the 1978 Tournament Series. MTA and TRC will be combined in a competitive format requiring both types of throws in future tournament series. (See Official Rules.)

MTA is unique among timed events. While the others try to reduce time toward zero, MTA seeks to expand it toward the infinite. In fact, both of these events exhibit a refreshingly new philosophy of field event play—a rapport between man and his implement and elements not found in track and field. Is it possible that the substitution of MTA and TRC for more traditional pastimes on the playground could instill in youngsters more awareness of nature and a more open concept of time and distance?

**Milking it. MTA catches should be caught right off the ground whenever possible.**

# 3. Double Disc Court

Probably a hundred different court games have been attempted with a disc. The back-and-forth nature of tossing a Frisbee disc reminds many people of tennis volleys, and they set out to devise a game around that observation. The disc does not lend itself well to court games: Nets don't work, throwing and catching don't provide as much continuity as batting a ball back and forth, and it is difficult to design a court that can facilitate top-level throwing as well as beginning.

Double Disc Court is the best example so far of a game that comes to grip with all these problems. In doing so, DDC fills an important need in Frisbee disc play: DDC is the only tournament sport suitable for one-to-one and pairs competition.

The game was developed by the redoubtable Jim Palmeri in Rochester, New York, in 1970. City championships were held in '71, '72, and '73. At the famous American Flying Disc Open in August 1974, singles DDC was a featured event, along with golf (see chapter 4). At that time the dimensions of the court were about one-third the present size, and it quickly became apparent the court was much too small. The competition disintegrated into a juggling match.

The game resurfaced at the 1976 Jersey Jam and again at the 1977 Philadelphia World Double Disc Court Championships. It was first used as a sanctioned event in the 1978 National Tournament Series. Its debut was met with much indifference, and several problems had to be remedied with rule changes as the season progressed. By the end of the season, appreciation for DDC had risen considerably.

DDC is not as typically American as the other disc sports. Game strategies are very subtle. The tensions of the game appear and dissolve again before any

**An ideal situation. When one player gets off a floater just as the other makes a catch, the second player can time a burn to score a double.**

but knowledgeable observers realize it. Play is relatively slow paced until scoring opportunities appear, and then there can be a flurry of activity.

PLAY

Three things are necessary for excellence in DDC:

*Flight Control.* Top-level play requires high floating shots; accurate curves; flat, fast burners; and gentle drop shots. Placement is everything. Competence with different delivery styles is advisable to avoid regripping between catch and throw. Spend a lot of practice time on the court getting a feel for the ranges of your throws and what it takes to keep them in the court.

*Court Sense.* You need a general ability to know where you and your partner are in the court, the positions of your opponents, where the disc will land and whether it is likely to travel out once it does, and what all of this means with regard to your next throw or catch.

*Communication.* Partners must keep each other informed. Experienced pairs understand each other's moves, which eliminates some talk, but failure to tell your partner what's on your mind can lead to dumb mistakes.

**Double Disc Court is sometimes a waiting game. However, if your team won the previous point, you must initiate throwing or you'll lose the next point.**

Sometimes a double can be avoided if the first disc can be tipped while the second disc is caught and returned. If both discs are touched at once, that's a double, so a tip will only work if the first disc to arrive is tipped.

**It's not sound strategy for both players to go for the same disc. It doesn't matter here since the burn already scored.**

Double Disc Court 37

**Keeping your eyes on the disc and on your opponents at the same time is a knack the DDC player must master.**

**Diving for the burn in the corner. Such burns have to be thrown with spin that will kick them back into the court.**

Time lag is the obvious key to pressuring the opposition and creating scoring opportunities. If you can escape getting doubled yourself you can return the problem to the opponent: Hold your disc until the last instant before the other disc arrives. Float your disc to the opponent's court while your partner waits for the right moment to deliver a burn.

On the throw-off, players usually opt for floaters or curves, trying to keep their throw up longer than the opponent's to gain a time edge. Remember, when

**With both discs on their way at once, the scramble is on. Communication between partners is essential.**

one team's throw plus catch plus return equals the other team's throw plus catch, a double occurs. The trick is to build up the time lag in your favor but not in such a way that you leave yourself open for a burn. Burns are sometimes attempted on the throw-off in an outright effort to score, and they are used as a last resort to gain a break when your first throw is obviously headed out, or when your teammate will not be able to catch the opposing team's throw.

# OFFICIAL RULES OF DOUBLE DISC COURT

## THE COURT

Two 12 by 12 meter courts marked out on grass and set 15 meters apart, measured from the front edge.

Throwing continues until a disc touches out-of-bounds or touches in a court.

## EQUIPMENT

Two discs of the same model. If competitors cannot come to agreement as to what model to use, two 119G World Class Frisbee discs are to be used.

## GENERAL PLAYING RULES

Two discs are used in play at the same time.

Each team of two players defends one court.

Each player attempts to throw a disc into his opponents' court such that it lands at an angle of 45 degrees or less to the ground, either side up, and stops without rolling or sliding out-of-bounds.

A player or team may never touch both discs at the same time or use a held disc to touch the other disc.

Each player may use one or both hands to catch any disc that threatens to land and stay inside the court.

The players must throw the disc from inside their respective court. A foot fault requires a rethrow if requested by the opponents.

A player may never touch his or her own throw or his or her teammate's throw.

After the throw-off, each throw must be made from the point on the court where the disc is caught. Normal momentum and throwing motion is acceptable but running or walking while holding the disc is not allowed. Travelling requires a rethrow if requested by the opponents. If the disc is caught out-of-bounds, it must be brought into the court at the nearest point before being rethrown.

## MODE OF PLAY

Each team stands inside their court and has possession of one disc.

Upon a signal from one of the nonthrowing players, play begins by a player from each team making the first throw simultaneous-

## FIELD LAYOUT

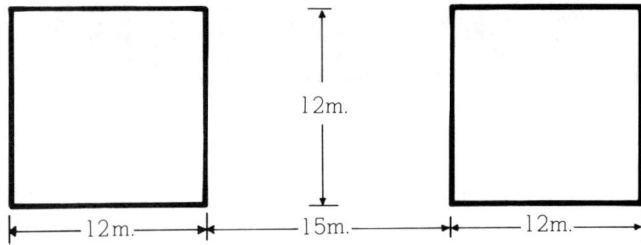

ly. Thereafter, until a point is scored or a "break" occurs, the players throw the discs at their discretion. The signal should be an even cadence count of "ready, two, one, throw" with release on the word "throw." The nonthrower from the team winning the previous point should call the cadence for the next exchange.

Team players must alternate first throws.

When a player on each team holds a disc and does not throw, creating an impasse situation, the team that won the previous point must initiate play immediately or lose the point.

Throwing continues until a disc touches the ground and stops dead. Throws released after that time count against the throwing team if they are thrown out. They cannot, however, score for the throwing team.

When play has stopped, and all thrown discs have come to rest, points are awarded.

## SCORING

Anytime a disc lands at an angle of 45 degrees or less to the ground inside the court area and comes to a dead stop before rolling or sliding out-of-bounds, a point is scored against the team defending that court. Throws landing at more than 45 degrees score against the team last touching the disc.

Anytime a disc touches any out-of-bounds area, a point is scored against the team which last touched that disc. Any further movement of the disc is of no consequence.

Anytime a player or team touches both discs at the same time during play two points are scored against that team.

If the discs make midair contact, a point is awarded to the opponent if a disc lands and remains in one team's court; two points are awarded to the opponent if both discs land and remain in one team's court. These are the only situations after midair contact in which a point or points can be scored.

## DEFINITION OF A BREAK

When both discs land and the result is a scoring situation against each team, a break occurs. No point is awarded and play is restarted.

## MISCELLANY

Before beginning play, the teams should flip a disc. Winner gets choice of court or choice of initiation. Loser must declare server.

Once a disc touches inside the court area, the defending players must not touch that disc until the point is determined or a break occurs. Violation results in loss of point for that disc or two points if a double disc situation occurs.

In the event the wind significantly affects the flight of the discs, the teams shall switch courts after every seven points (total) are accumulated.

For tournament play, there should be an observer for each team's court to call foot faults, double discs, and 45 degree landings.

Usual tournament play matches are two out of three games to fifteen points, win by two. Serving combinations should switch for each game. That is, if player A served against player B in game one, A should serve against player C in game two. Also, the winner of game one shall initiate play for the first point of game two of the match, and likewise for game three should the game be necessary.

For indoor or other hard surface play, 2 inch by 2 inch strips of wood may be used as lines. In this case, the disc may touch the wood but not slide or roll over the boundary.

For a game that moves so slowly, DDC requires enormous concentration. This is largely because it runs counter to so many of the usual playing sensibilities. For instance, you will usually want to deliver your softest throw precisely at those times when you are under the most pressure to get off a throw. Deciding whether a descending disc will land in your court or not is hard enough; it's nearly impossible when you also have to see if your partner is about to deliver or receive a throw. Often you have to hold in check your natural desire to make a catch until the last instant before the disc lands.

It takes about eight or ten games just to get comfortable with the rules and another fifteen or twenty games to get bad throws and "boo-boos" out of your system, and another fifteen or twenty games to de-

**Watching one over, hoping it'll hit the line.**

**A common DDC tactic is to burn the disc at the feet of an opponent who is holding the disc. In such cases, the thrower's partner will need to cover.**

**Scorekeepers are handy in tournament play.**

velop heads-up, strategic play. In other words, you have to give DDC a pretty good chance—don't give up on it too soon.

## FUTURE

DDC is perfectly suited for coed play. Like tennis, it is also a very social game which lends itself to pleasant repartee without sacrificing high level play. Watch for disc country clubs!

One rule change which may occur is omission of a point on a dropped or missed disc, since that greatly increases the possibility of a double anyway. The 1979 Tournament Series will tell much more about where Double Disc Court is headed.

**The upside-down backhand hangs well and drops straight, making it a valuable throw for DDC.**

# 4. Golf

Disc golf resembles a ball sport more obviously than any other disc sport. The roots of the game go back a long way, and, curiously, the refinements in the game over the years have increased the similarities to its ball counterpart. Spud Melin of Wham-O recalls that a golflike betting game was the first played with Wham-O's Pluto Platter in the '50s. "Holes" were made up spontaneously but were rarely more than two throws away.

· The first major competitive play was in 1969 at the IFA California meet held in Brookside Park, Pasadena. Jay Shelton won that event in which the putt had to hit below a ribbon tied around a tree, lamppost, or whatever. Credit for the first permanent course goes to George Sappenfield, who established one in Thousand Oaks, California.

The first national competition came in 1974. Octad featured an eighteen-hole course using ribboned trees as holes. Later in the summer, Jim Palmeri hosted the first American Flying Disc Open in Rochester, New York. The first disc-retaining holes—low boxes on the ground—were unveiled. And the biggest prize ever, a new car, went to Dan Roddick, who won by thirteen "strokes." Octad '75 experimented with circular ground receptacles fashioned from gardening fence.

In August 1976, after long negotiation, the Los Angeles County Park Board permitted Ed Headrick to set up a semi-permanent course at Oak Grove Park in La Canada, California, for use in the 1976 World Frisbee disc Championships. Tee boxes were marked off with split logs and four-inch pipes were sunk into the ground for the holes. Originally, it was intended that the course would come down after the

**Some putting styles look rather unorthodox.**

Championships, but as many as two thousand people a weekend were playing the course. Park officials, quick to recognize a good thing, decided the course should remain available to the public.

The volume of play stayed phenomenally high, and that spurred Headrick to develop the Disc Pole Hole™ and to found the Disc Golf Association. Since the unruliest fringe areas of a park are usually best suited to disc golf, and since an eighteen-hole Pole Hole course costs about the same as a jumbo swing set while providing amusement for ten times as many people, parks all over the world have been installing permanent courses.

## COURSE DESIGN

Still, a commitment to the game must exist among a goodly number of people before a Pole Hole course is feasible. There's nothing to stop you from designing your own course. In fact, many communities now have Pole Hole courses because an enterprising local club laid out a course that caught on and created popular demand.

You can use any number of targets for holing out, from natural objects to stakes or baskets. Let your ingenuity be your guide, but don't let it get the best

**A perfectly good round of golf can be played using only backhands.**

**However, there will be times when a backhand just won't do. More experienced golfers will know a variety of deliveries.**

**In golf, the mental game is just as important as the physical game. Here Ken Westerfield concentrates on his next shot as he walks to his disc.**

of you—there are several design considerations you should take into account: Your target should accept approach shots well enough that players will be encouraged to "go for it" from reasonable ranges, but it should not accept them so well that the challenge is gone. Putts of thirty feet or more should be an occasional possibility, a ten-foot putt should not be a "gimme." Targets that do not retain the disc can lead to disputes over whether a putt was successful or not—a minor problem. More importantly, they don't demand a putting "touch"—putts can be slammed home. Also, nobody wants flimsy, distracting receptacles left on public property. Your targets should be discrete and not interfere with land use or maintenance.

Some guidelines to keep in mind as you design the whole course are

• Provide challenges and risks. A course with no "disasters" is a bore. Make golfers pay for their errors.

• Avoid random punishment. Each shot should have a reasonable possibility of succeeding. Forcing play through a thicket is a test of luck, not skill.

• Provide opportunities for a range of throws, from long, full-out flights to short or curving chip shots.

• Have an even mix of left- and right-curving fairways.

• Use natural obstacles to their fullest; for in-

**When stretching around an obstacle, the planted foot must be the closest to the pole.**

stance, cement slabs make great slide traps.
- Avoid walkways, playgrounds, and picnic areas that get much use.
- Design holes that demand not only long drives but also accurate placement for the second shot. The extent to which poor placement goes unpunished is known as the "forgivingness" of the course, and a course should not have too much or too little.

TECHNIQUE

Golf demands both the least and the most throwing versatility. You can play a creditable round using only one style of delivery, but for that competitive edge you will want to be competent with just about

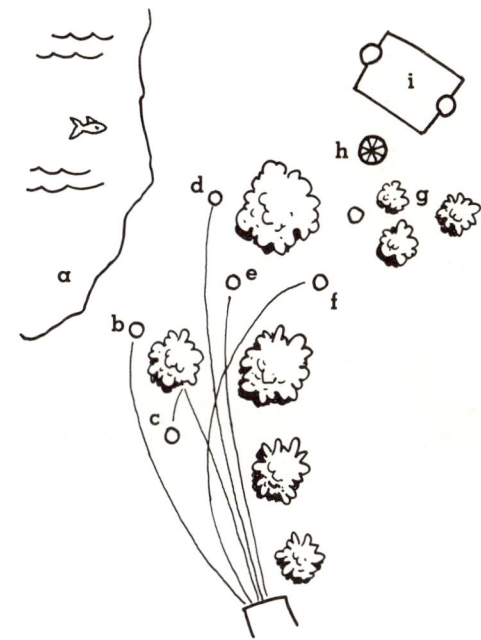

The design of a disc golf course. (a.) An out-of-bounds area for throws carried off by the wind. (b.) Playing it safe is punished by inferior position. (c.) Inaccurate tee shots are punished. (d.) Estimation of range is required—throws too short or long are punished. (e.) A good drive. (f.) A superior player has a chance for an outstanding drive if willing to take the risk. (g.) Approach shot obstacles. (h.) The Disc Pole Hole. (i.) A cement slab makes a great slide trap.

College campuses are excellent locations for disc golf courses. Distinctive campus features can be used to require distinctive throws.

every throw ever devised. This quality makes golf the best training ground for beginning and intermediate players. After getting comfortable with the game, they can begin adding new techniques to their repertoire at their own pace.

Eventually, most top golfers develop the ability to handle each of the following requirements, often with two or more different delivery styles:
- long drives of sixty to ninety meters or more
- skips with both spins
- a variety of rollers with both spins
- a super-accurate putting throw.

The throwing skills needed for these demanding tasks often take years to develop fully. In addition to throwing skills themselves, golfers must also develop an effective perspective on the game. Many very skilled throwers are only fair golfers because of their approach to the game. What is required is an ability to evaluate play situations and then come up with the appropriate throws. This process is conservative by nature, but some risks must be taken to achieve excellent results, that is, risky flights must be taken, but only when the odds are sufficiently in favor of success and the long-run rewards outweigh the hazards.

The types of shots made in a round of golf can be broken down into three categories: drives and fairway shots, approach shots, and putts. Drives require maximum distance plus optimum placement. Approach shots require appropriate distance and great lateral accuracy. Acceptable putting position is the goal, and sometimes a shot on the target itself is possible without sacrificing that goal.

Putting requirements vary depending on the type

**Rollers are commonly used for drives and approach shots. Variations in the angle, speed, and spin of the delivery can produce rollers that will wind their way through almost any arrangement of obstacles.**

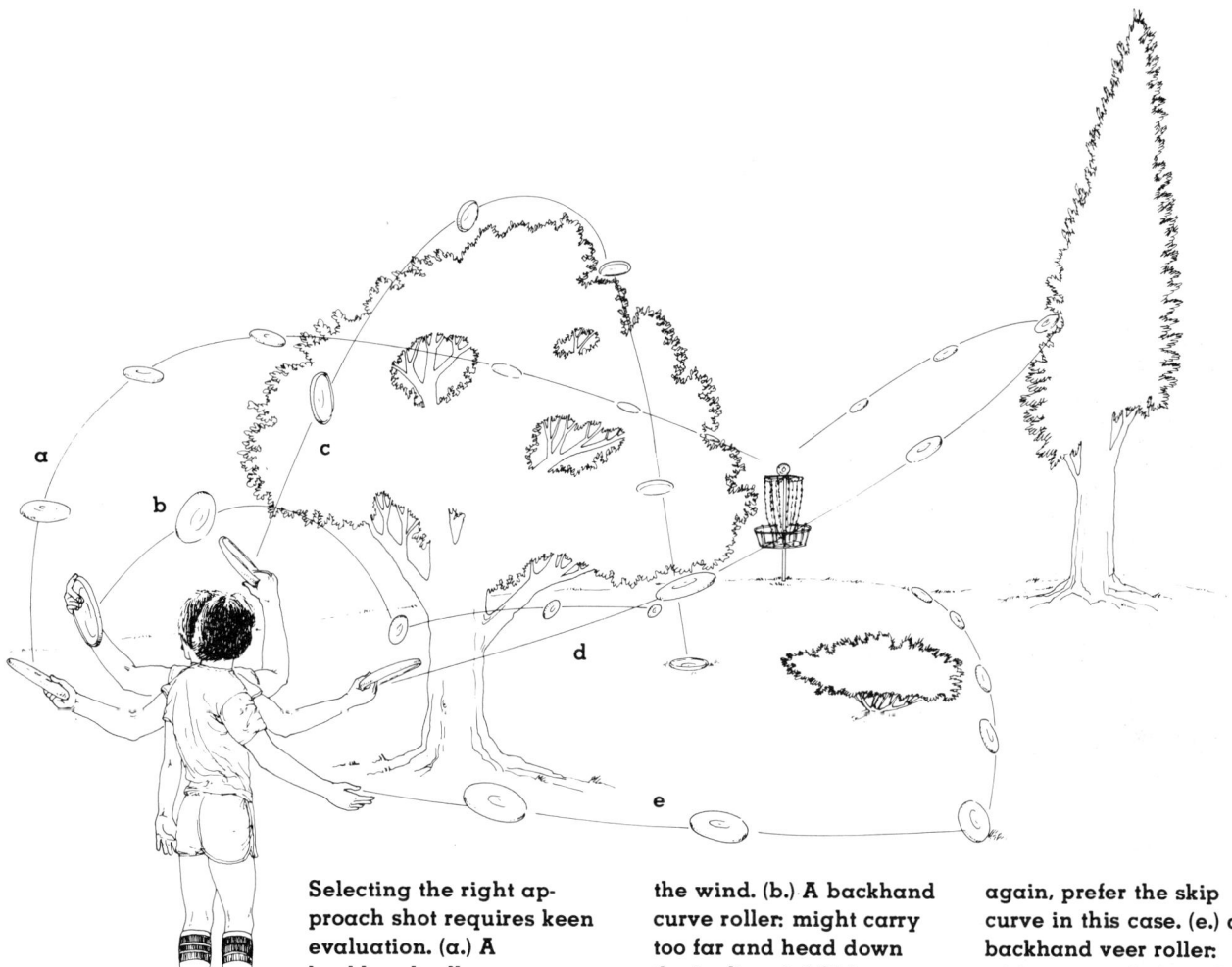

Selecting the right approach shot requires keen evaluation. (a.) A backhand roll curve or a sidearm skip curve: the backhand might roll down the incline after landing—prefer the sidearm depending on the wind. (b.) A backhand curve roller: might carry too far and head down the incline. (c.) Sidearm lob: probably won't carry far enough because of the height of the tree. (d.) Sidearm roll curve or backhand skip curve: again, prefer the skip curve in this case. (e.) a backhand veer roller: with a ground obstacle, might not be able to cut it back sharply enough to reach the Pole Hole.

## OFFICIAL RULES OF GOLF

General–Disc golf is played like ball golf using a flying disc. One point is counted each time the disc is thrown and when a penalty is incurred. The object is to acquire the lowest score.

Tee Throws–Tee throws must be released from within 2 meters behind the designated tee line.

Lie–The spot on or directly underneath the point where the previous throw landed is the lie.

Throwing Order–After teeing off the player whose disc is farthest from the hole throws first. The player with the lowest number of throws on the previous hole is the first to tee off on the next hole.

Fairway Throws–Fairway throws must be made with the foot closest to the hole *on* the lie at the moment of release. The other foot may be no closer to the hole than the lie. A run-up and normal follow-through are allowed.

Dog Leg–A dog leg is one or more designated trees or poles in the fairway that must be passed on a designated side when approaching the hole. Until the dog leg is passed, placement of the player's free foot may be no closer to the dog leg than the lie.

Putt Throw–Within 10 meters of the hole, a player may not step past the lie in making the putt throw. Falling or jumping putts are not allowed.

Unplayable Lie–Any disc that comes to rest more than 2 meters above the ground is considered an unplayable lie. After declaring an unplayable lie the disc must be thrown from a new lie on the ground, directly beneath the unplayable lie. An unplayable lie incurs a one-throw penalty.

Out-of-Bounds–A throw that lands out of bounds must be played from the point where the disc went out of bounds. Water hazards and public roads are always out of bounds. An out-of-bounds throw incurs a one-throw penalty.

Course Courtesy–Don't throw until players ahead of you are out of range.

Practice Throws–Absolutely no practice throws between the time of initial drive and final putt. The first instance will result in a warning. Subsequent instances will result in an automatic one-throw penalty for each infraction.

No Falling Putts–Players stepping in front of their lie immediately after the putting motion will be warned once and made to rethrow the shot if the violating putt was successful. Subsequent infractions will result in a one-throw penalty and rethrow in each instance.

Mark All Lies–A disc must be used to indicate the location of each lie. All lies, no matter how close to the hole, must be marked and thrown.

Accurate foot placement on lies and tees will be expected and violators will be warned once and then penalized one throw for each subsequent infraction.

**The proper way to mark your lie. First, place a second disc next to the disc you threw in line with the pole (or dog leg, if there is one between you and the pole). Second, remove your first disc and place your foot on the spot. For long approach shots, you may run up to your lie, but your throw must be made with your foot behind the marker disc.**

of target. Disc Pole Holes are the most difficult since the putt must have the correct speed, spin, and angle when it hits. Unfortunately, even some apparently perfect putts kick out of the basket. Ed Headrick has put in a lot of work on the weight and arrangement of the chains to overcome that problem. The latest model Pole Holes rarely lose a good putt.

Typical drive shots are long, straight or curving backhands or sidearms. Often, straight and curve rollers are used. Approach shots commonly used are backhand and sidearm straight throws, skips, hovers, roll and skip curves, and rollers. Occasionally, you'll see wrist flips, veer rollers, upside-down lobs, or even multiple skips. The best putt is the one that works best for you. For most, it is the negative-angle backhand. Push shots, butterflies, sidearms, spinners, and other throws are also employed.

Golf has the special attraction of providing an objective measure of progress. Many factors contribute to the final score of a round, but the numbers say it all.

## FUTURE

No disc game rivals golf for appeal to the general playing public. Some reasons for the lure of this sport:
- the concept is easy to grasp
- success is possible at all levels of skill, for all ages and all levels of physical condition
- cost for the player is very low

- the strategic challenges exceed those of the popular ball-and-club version of the game because the disc player has a greater variety of options when overcoming obstacles, and there are also many more obstacles on the course
- relatively little space is required for a disc course

**A butterfly putt.**

**Getting back into the fairway.**

**A spin-off putt.**

- it televises excellently as you can actually see the flight, and the strategic thinking of the players is apparent
- it is an excellent format for both making and gauging progress in disc-throwing skills
- the playing skills carry over to other disc sports. sports.

Golf will be the central activity of the commercial

**A backhand curve putt.**

# Golf 51

## RELATED GAMES

*Call-your-hole golf.* This was the earliest form of the game and is played the same except there is an extra element of strategy. That is the winner of each hole makes up the next one. Obviously, the idea is to pick a layout suited to your talents. If you are the best distance thrower in the group, you'd choose a target that required two or three long shots. Finesse throwers will try to wind their way through trees and shrubs. The best hover thrower will make the target something you have to land on top of. Whether you choose a one-par hole or an eight-par doesn't matter—whatever your imagination comes up with.

*Speed Golf.* This is great for a rollicking good time. The rules are the same as golf, but your score is a product both of the number of throws you take and how long it takes you to finish the course. In a twenty-player pool, a player who finished first in strokes and third in time would receive twenty and eighteen points respectively, for a total of thirty-eight.

**An upside-down sidearm putt.**

**A negative-attitude backhand putt, probably the surest of all putts. Make the putt with an upward stroke from waist level to chest level so that the disc tilts forward and noses into the chains.**

disc club in the future. It will become a common feature of recreational facilities nationwide and attract large numbers of serious competitors and commercial sponsors. Wait and see. Better yet, grab your disc bag and head out to the links.

# 5. Freestyle

Freestyle play, almost by definition, was the first disc game. Play catch, *then* invent games. Every game of toss is freestyle because the players do what they wish in the situation.

Fred Morrison, who invented the plastic flying disc, dazzled crowds simply with the flight of the disc. He drew lots of "oohs" and "aahs" for curves, skips, and behind-the-back and fingertip catches. That may sound simple by today's standards, but those early demonstrators were considered magicians. The secrets of these tricks were printed on the early disc packages, and freestyle went public.

With the arrival of the Pro model Frisbee disc and, particularly, the Super-Pro in the '60s, the great exploration began. Progress was slow because there was little effective communication and no good analogies to follow. Wrist flips and tipping may seem obvious now, but such ideas developed slowly.

Leading pockets of development were in Berkeley, Laguna Beach, and at a few Eastern colleges. Laguna Beach led in flowing play and the first full-handed "tips." Berkeley developed a very fast, skipping, long-distance game with spinning catches and varied throws. Eastern play centered around a competitive, trick-catch game that promoted consistent catching and accurate throwing.

The lines of communication that sped the development of freestyle emerged in 1973 when informal freestyle appeared at the International Frisbee Tournament, and as a major event at the Toronto Championship. The race was on to get hot. Ken Westerfield and Jim Kenner, a Canadian team, won the competition. They became the first independent commercial team, working the streets of Toronto as their first job.

**The air bounce, along with the tip, started freestyle off in its present direction about 1973.**

Getting hyperspin (maximum rotation of the disc) requires a hard snap of the elbow and wrist. The more spin, the easier continuation moves are.

The dream shot, as performed by John "Dreamer" Weyand himself, started the interest in upside-down throws for freestyle.

By 1975, freestyle was a major event at several meets. The team of Irv Kalb and Dan Roddick swept the U.S., Canadian, Octad, and World titles. The floodgates opened in 1976 as dozens of teams contended for the freestyle titles.

As an insight into the level of play at that first meet, there was no brushing and nothing approaching a delay. Triumphs of the meet included a knee trap by Westerfield, a twenty-tip series by Irv Kalb, and an amazing catch-of-his-own-throw by Bruce Koger as he threw to Dan Roddick, who tipped it until Bruce arrived to catch it between his legs. Dynamite stuff at the time!

The following year, John Kirkland introduced the air bounce, Kerry Kolmar introduced delays and brushing, and Ken Westerfield presented body rolls.

The upside-down wrist flip is perhaps the most versatile upside-down throw for freestyle. Here, with a left-handed delivery, it becomes a counter-spin throw.

## PLAY

Players who thrive on competition should dive in. Most players, though, will find it beneficial to let their individual style mature away from competition's pressure for a while. Several exceptional freestylers don't compete at all, and that may be your choice too. The question is, does competition make you feel better or worse about your game?

Recreationally or competitively, many playing tools are needed. The terminology we have selected for grouping these tools reflects the fact that the skills have become too diverse to be contained by old terms such as "throw" or "catch."

**The variety component in freestyle judging puts pressure on players to come up with new twists to old throws. Here is a between-the-legs blind staker.**

**The upside-down backhand is the preferred counter spin upside-down throw.**

*Propulsions.* For good variety you need all the standard throws, and at least one throw of each spin direction you can deliver with very high rotation (heavy Z's, as it's called). You should never have to regrip to throw. Accurate control of skips, curves, rollers, and flight attitude in general is crucial. A variety of upside-down deliveries is essential. Non-throw propulsions, such as twirls and kick brushes, have been gaining in popularity.

*Continuations.* The delay has become the premier tool of play. It is a must. In fact, delaying both spins with either hand is becoming a must. Tipping control is vital. Midflight attitude controls (MAC's) are seen more and more frequently, particularly in three-player freestyle.

*Accelerations.* Airbrushing is central to the modern game, as it provides both controlled movement of the play and acceleration of spin. Twirling and padiddling can be used to recover spin, and they make for some unique moves. These last two categories, continuations and accelerations, are often called discwork or "tricking" the disc.

*Terminations.* Even in today's top freestyle you will see an occasional "catch." Actually, the art is underdeveloped (since players are more intrigued with continuation moves), and few players have an adequate range of closing moves. Players should also be more aware that terminations can define the rhythm of their play: trailing-edge catches that blend into a return throw keep the tempo lively; a knee trap might be used to cap a stunning series of continuation moves and thus give time for their impact to be felt. More creativity is called for.

**The key to prolonged discwork is lubrication. Armor All and several silicone sprays are the lubricants of choice; however, some non-water-soluble silicone sprays have recently been implicated in nerve damage to the finger. Be careful to choose water-soluble silicone sprays.**

**In 1973, being able to tip at all would rack up freestyle points. Now fancy variations are needed to impress the judges.**

**A chin tip. This is really stretching it to please the judges.**

One way to conceive of freestyle is that the disc can exist in a number of spin states, can move in any direction in any attitude, and can move in a wide range of speeds, all of which contribute to a total energy state. The spin states are clock spinning, counter spinning, twirling, rolling, and dead. Freestyle moves are designed to maintain energy states and especially to make transitions to other energy states. A chest roll takes a spinning disc and turns it into a rolling disc; a puddle catch at the end turns it into a twirling disc; flip it off your finger into a delay and you have spin again. When dead discs drop, they helix (rock). At some point in the descent the disc will be perfectly aligned for a brush, thanks to the helixing motion. That is known as the Zeno point,

**A cross-legged foot tip.**

**A double foot tip.**

**A heel tip.**

and a foot brush then will turn the dead disc into a flying, spinning disc. A turnover changes a disc from right side up to upside-down and changes the effective spin at the same time. Careful counter brushing can change clock spin to counter, and vice versa. Theoretically, there should be at least one control move to get the disc from any energy state to any other you desire. If that's true, many moves remain to be worked out.

**Some delay moves require precision control and fine adjustment of the disc.**

The most productive way to acquire freestyle skills is to focus on a few at a time. Drill them until you get the general feel, then blend them into your play to keep from getting weary of the repetition. You might, for instance, practice delays when you get clock-spin hovers, blind catches when throws arrive at the right height, and hyperspin wrist flips when you move close enough to your partner. Other than those special cases, you play your regular game. Soon, those moves are part of your regular game.

Setting the disc up for yourself is invaluable in learning continuation moves. If you do not yet know how to perform a setup, you would do well to invest some time in learning (See FBTM, p. 119). You can get a lot of discwork practice in a short time with setups, and it gives you something to do at those times when you feel like playing but can't find a partner.

In general, play is developing in the direction of dance. Top players will soon find dance training essential for rapid progress. Martial arts and gymnastics could also make valuable contributions to playing style.

**Working a delay in tight quarters is one way to emphasize to the judges that you have absolute control.**

*Co-oping.* The cooperative aspect of freestyle has always been important, but with the advancement of play it has become an even more integral feature. Co-oping comes in two forms. In the first, a break tipper sets the disc up with MAC's, tips, body skips, deflections, or tunnels to one or more partners playing to the rear. In the second, two or more players (one of whom might be the break tipper joining in) work jointly on delay and tipping moves, brushes, body rolls, and Siamese catches.

Good co-op requires an advanced level of accurate control because of the necessity of working with others. Playing solo, you can limit the range of play to fit your limitations. In co-op, you can be plunged abruptly into challenging situations. Your partner might pass you a delay or brush with the "wrong spin." You might expect a MAC and get a tunnel with little time to react. In short, the key to cooperative play is communication and understanding between partners. The better cooperative players make their partners look good, not only because of their great playing skills, but also because they create interesting situations for their partners within their skill levels. They position well when their partner has the disc, and they keep their partner informed of their intentions. They have, you might say, learned to cooperate.

**A double-legover delay transfer**

## JUDGING

Judging has been a major issue since the beginning of competitive play. At one extreme are players who feel it is profane to judge freestyle at all. At the other extreme are players who have worked out minutely detailed difficulty ratings and scoring systems. The one distinctive feature all the scoring systems have had in common is that the players do the judging. Here is the historical progression of judging systems:

1. Each judge ranks all teams.
2. Each judge gives a 1-to-10 score to each team.
3. Each judge scores each team 1 to 10 on each of Variety, Execution, and Difficulty.
4. Judges are assigned to a single component for which they assign each team a 1-to-10 score.
5. Mathematical systems are devised to quantify and objectify each category, and subjective categories such as "flow" are added.

Debate still rages, with some players lacking con-

**The ultimate in delay control: a toe delay.**

**The ability to move to a rim delay and then recover back to a center delay is necessary for executing a behind-the-back delay transfer.**

fidence in the sensitivity of mathematical systems, but demanding "objectivity." It would be hard to demonstrate that anything has been gained by the increasingly complex systems, and in fact, the increasing complexity of freestyle itself may force a return to the first simple systems. Perhaps unbiased and educated subjectivity will prove to be the best evaluation.

**Always a spectacular move, a well-executed chest roll is a crowd pleaser.**

**An upside-down chest roll is much trickier than the right side-up version.**

**A back roll is not particularly difficult itself, but recovering to make a catch or continuation move off a back roll is.**

# Freestyle

The turnover is the latest innovation in freestyle. To accomplish it, the player must be able to handle both spins with either hand. In order to turn the disc from one side up to the other, a player has to move precisely with the precessional and gyroscopic forces acting on the disc.

## FREESTYLE JUDGING STANDARDS

Over the years, consensus has developed that four major components can be used to represent our values in a freestyle routine. They are: Execution, Difficulty, Variety, and Presentation.

### DIFFICULTY

High difficulty scores are awarded to routines in which the demonstrated moves require a high degree of skill to perform. Routines in which a smaller portion of difficult moves are demonstrated are scored correspondingly lower.

Any system designed for transforming the observed difficulty into a numerical score is dependent upon assigning generally agreed upon difficulty ratings to each of the basic individual moves used in a routine.

The underlying principle used for assigning a difficulty rating to these basic moves is the relative length of time it takes for the average player to develop that move. What must be avoided is the tendency to rate the difficulty of a move in terms of personal ability to do that particular move. While it is just as easy for an accomplished player to delay a disc as it is to simply catch it with one hand, it is obvious that much more practice time was spent learning the delay than was spent learning to catch a disc with one hand. That fact alone determines that the delay is a more difficult move than a one-handed catch. The ease with which a move is performed does not determine the difficulty; it is the practice time required by the typical player to develop that ease which is the determining factor.

Any of the possible moves can be classified into a difficulty range of 0 to 5. A zero rating is reserved for the very basic no-difficulty moves such as a straightforward one or two-handed grab. A five rating is reserved for only the most outstandingly difficult moves.

Judges must record a rating ranging from 0 to 5 for each move of a routine as it occurs. At the end of the routine, all the recorded values are totaled and that sum is divided by the total number of moves that were rated. The resulting average is then multiplied by three, the present difficulty constant. The end result is a score ranging from 0 to 10 points. A score above 10 is numerically possible but not probable in terms of current freestyle skills.

## SCORING PROCEDURE

1. As each propulsion and playing move is observed, a rating ranging from 0 to 5 for that move is recorded on the scoresheet.

2. Throws that do not reach their intended destination are not rated for difficulty and are not recorded as a move.

3. Flights that are dropped before any playing moves are completed are not rated for difficulty and are not recorded as a move.

4. Flights that are dropped after one or more playing moves have been successfully completed are rated for difficulty on the basis of the moves performed before the drop occurs (see judging notes).

5. Score computation:

    a. The values of all the rated moves are totaled.

    b. This total is divided by the number of moves that were given a rating.

    c. The resulting number is multiplied by three. The overall result is the difficulty score.

    d. If the final result is over 10, the score is recorded as 10.

Beyond the developmental-time consideration, other general factors contribute to the judges' estimation of the difficulty of each move. Many of these rely on the judges' knowledge of play and experience, which must be extensive, particularly at higher levels of play.

**Turnovers are difficult enough. A turnover into an elbow delay has to be one of the trickiest moves going.**

**Controlling the disc by pushing with the nail against the outside rim is variously known as a guide, a push, or a hesitation.**

# Freestyle 63

**Air brushing is the handiest way to add spin to a disc so that discwork can be prolonged.**

**A puddle catch, or upside-down finger twirling catch, requires precision contact with the disc.**

## JUDGING NOTES

Scoring the difficulty category requires judges who are very familiar with all the commonly used moves and are able to recognize them quickly for what they are as they are being performed.

Some things to look for when scoring difficulty:
1. High leaps, twisting leaps, and contortions greatly influence the difficulty value of basic trick catches.

2. Care must be taken to distinguish "cosmetic" moves, such as flips, handstands, etc., which are completed well before or after the disc arrives from those moves which shortly precede the arrival of the disc, adding to the difficulty of the catch by lessening visual contact/reaction time.

3. Each throw is rated for difficulty as an individual move. The judge must take into account the situation in which the throw is made as well as the particular type of throw itself. For instance, an immediate rethrow from a contorted position increases the difficulty, and that should be reflected in the rating.

Each playing move is rated as a unit that extends from the point where the disc is first touched to the point where it is terminated or transferred. The individual moves within a combination move are rated as a unit taken together. Separate ratings are not recorded for each of the moves that compose a co-op or combination move.

In the event of a drop, all the moves successfully completed before the drop occurs are rated as a unit taken together. The fact that the disc is dropped does not affect the difficulty value of that successfully completed unit. The particular move directly involved in the drop, such as an attempted catch or a bad foot tip, is not considered part of the completed unit, and does not affect the difficulty rating of the successfully completed unit.

A flight on which no move at all is successfully completed before the drop is not rated for difficulty. In terms of judging difficulty, it is interpreted as no move having been done at all and is not recorded on the difficulty scoresheet in any manner.

**Just catching the disc isn't enough anymore. "Terminations" require gymnastic positioning.**

**The triple-fake, or cross-body blind catch, is still a crowd pleaser, particularly as performed here on an upside-down throw.**

## VARIETY

All freestyle play can be classified into three basic modes of action. These are propulsion, continuation, and termination. Each category includes many specific disc/body actions or "moves" but all the moves in each category share important similarity:

*Propulsion* is the impartation of spin to the disc. Directional movement may also, but need not, occur. Examples: throws, setups, brushes, and twirls from nonspinning state.

*Continuation* involves two subcategories: (1) *Maintenance* moves include any which affect or use the flight or spin of the disc without adding spin. Examples: delays, tips, deflections, rolls, tunnels, MAC's or turnovers. (2) *Acceleration* moves include any which add to the existing spin of the disc. Examples: brushes, twirls, hyperspins.

A *termination* is any move which stops the spin of the disc. Examples: catches, traps, freezes, or drops.

The variety scoring system is based on the number of different moves observed in each of these modes of action.

## SCORING PROCEDURE

Each move, when shown for the first time in a routine, should be entered as 1.0 under the appropriate category. Subsequent uses of the same move should be given notations from 0 to 1.0 depending how different that use is from previous uses. For example, the first instance of a delay on the right hand would be worth a full 1.0. Later right-hand delays would have to be somehow different to be awarded points. Taking the delay behind the back or under the leg would justify another 1.0. Exact repetition scores 0. Slight variations would result in the midrange scores (.1 to .9).

This system provides a method of scoring variety that does not depend on mandating certain moves or types of moves that must be performed in order to get a perfect score. Each group of

# Freestyle

competitors is totally free to do the moves they prefer to do and still has the opportunity to score as high in variety as any other competitor.

Accurate judging requires full concentration, good short-term recall and sensitivity to significant variations.

The final score is generated by taking the sum of all the points recorded on the score sheet and multiplying it by 0.15. A result over 10 is recorded as 10.0.

## JUDGING NOTES

1. First and foremost, variety is *not* execution. It does not matter whether a throwing move or termination move is successful; what counts is whether a particular move occurs or not. When judging variety, each different move performed is given credit, even if the move is not successfully executed. If a between-the-legs trail catch is attempted, and has not been performed previously in the routine, then variety credit is given whether or not the disc is actually caught. Execution judges will take care of how well the move is performed; variety judges are concerned only with the fact that a move has occurred.

2. When determining throwing variety, the grip, the delivery motion and the trajectory are all taken into account. If any combination of these factors is different from any previous throw performed, the throw is considered different. For example, a fan-gripped backhand air bounce is different from a fan-gripped backhand straight throw. The only time a throw is considered a repeat is when all three factors are the same as used in a previous throw.

**Flamingo catches were among the new moves introduced by Canadian players in 1977. There are several variations to this basic flamingo, and all are spectacular.**

**Constorksion moves dramatically display a player's ability to read the disc's flight precisely. Here is an under-the-leg trail catch.**

**Another version of the under-the-leg trail.**

**Another constorksion move: a catch between crossed legs.**

3. A continuation move that is used to take control of a disc from flight is different from the same move performed after the disc has been taken under control. Each different control-taking continuation move is awarded the full 1.0 variety credit. Example: A foot tip applied to a disc in flight is recorded as a different move from a foot tip set up after the disc is under control and is awarded the full 1.0 variety credit.

4. A MAC or tunnel is considered a continuation move. Each different way a flight is MAC'ed or tunneled gives the move full variety credit.

5. A sequence of moves done cooperatively is considered to be different from the same sequence done by an individual.

6. Moves done with one spin are different from moves done with the opposite spin and are given partial to full variety credit.

7. Moves done with a crown-down disc are different from those with a crown-up disc and are given partial to full variety credit.

8. Different sequences of the same acceleration or continuation moves are given variety credit, partial or full, depending upon how different the sequence is.

EXECUTION

The guiding question of this component is "How well did the players perform the moves they attempted?"

Three levels of deduction are possible for any execution which is less than perfect:

3 point—major error such as a wild throw, a dropped catching attempt, or any other significant disruption of play.

2 point—moderate errors such as erratic but completed throws, obviously broken combinations, desperation moves, or low difficulty terminations such as trapped or two-handed saves.

1 point—minor errors such as bobbles, stumbling recoveries, momentary loss of control, clumsy regripping, or other detracting flaws.

Freestyle 67

**Some constorksion moves leave no choice but to crash into the ground.**

**A between-the-legs catch is turned into something a little more spectacular.**

**A knee trap is an intriguing way to terminate the disc.**

A deduction should be noted for each error as it occurs. Care should be exercised to apply the same standard for each routine.

At the conclusion of the routine, all the deductions should be added together and then subtracted from 100. The result is then divided by 10 and is the initial score.

Step 1: 3+2+1+3+3+1+2+1+3+3+3+3 = 28
Step 2: 100 − 28 = 72
Step 3: 72/10 = 7.2

After all routines have been performed and given an initial score, the judges may wish to add or subtract a constant from all scores. For instance, a five-minute final routine has more opportunity for deduction than a three-minute preliminary, so the judges may wish to add equally to the longer routines to bring the scores into the expected range.

Step 4: 7.2 + 1.3 [constant] = 8.5

JUDGING NOTES

1. Execution judges must avoid determining their scores solely on the basis of the number of drops and bad throws recorded. The deductions for drops reflect the amount of major technical errors committed, and this is only a part of scoring for execution. Two routines with an identical number of drops could be greatly different in their overall execution, and to score them the same because they had the same number of drops would be a great injustice. All factors of execution as outlined in the standards must be taken into account.

2. It is very important to avoid the practice of adjusting the execution deduction for drops according to the ratio of the total number of throws performed. This common misconception is based on the premise that more throws in a routine mean more opportunity for dropping a disc, and this leads to the thought that bigger deductions should be made for drops in a routine that has fewer throws than in a routine with more throws.

A reverse ankle trap scores high in the difficulty ratings.

Working two discs requires supreme concentration.

This thinking is in error because it does not take into account what happens to the disc in the time between throws. The important factor is that the time from the first throw to the end of the routine is the same for all competitors, and whether the routine consists of 40 quick throws and catches or 10 throws with 10 long, involved combination moves, the disc is handled for the same amount of time and the opportunities to drop the disc are the same.

Any attempt by players to reduce the dropping opportunity by holding the disc between throws is an unwise use of performance time, and is dealt with by deductions for pauses and hesitations.

PRESENTATION

This component is the most subjective of the four aspects of Freestyle judging. A score of 1 (poor) to 10 (excellent) is awarded each group based on the personal evaluation of each judge. There are, however, some guiding issues which are to be considered in that judgment:

1. *Flow:* Did the play have pleasing continuity and pace? If music was used, did the routine utilize that background effectively?

2. *Entertainment:* Did the play produce an enjoyable experience for the viewer? Did the players communicate effectively with the audience through their play?

3. *Creativity:* Did the routine demonstrate an inventive approach to play?

These three major elements should be reflected in the presentation score. They are inevitably related to the other components in at least an indirect way, but judges should consider these elements as independently as possible.

# Freestyle

## FUTURE

One is tempted to assert smugly that all the possible freestyle skills have already been discovered, but that is to invite egg on the face. The history of discovery indicates new breakthrough moves will be uncovered. But there is already more to freestyle than can be assimilated; the richness of current play is incredible. The best routines provide a phantasmagoric display of both subtle and obvious variations on the simple theme of throw and catch. High-rotation throws and lubricated discs make continuation and acceleration moves possible that were be-

**Padiddles go places delays never dared. Here Jim Brown executes "the seal" with a padiddle.**

## CO-OPING

A chest roll through a tunnel to a between-the-legs catch.

It's always a good idea to start a freestyle routine by getting the support of the crowd.

Air brushing is an excellent way to get the disc to your co-op partner with plenty of spin on it.

A break tipper adjusts the attitude of the disc for the back-up player.

Here the second leg of a cross-leg kick tip belongs to a partner.

Freestyle 71

A co-op turnover.

Simultaneous moves are one way of letting the judges know you have your act together.

A shoulder roll to a knee trap.

## Frisbee Disc Sports and Games

**A double, double chest roll.**

**Siamese catches are frequently used to cap off a series of co-oping moves.**

**A triple chest roll.**

Freestyle 73

Some three-player co-op moves get rather involved.

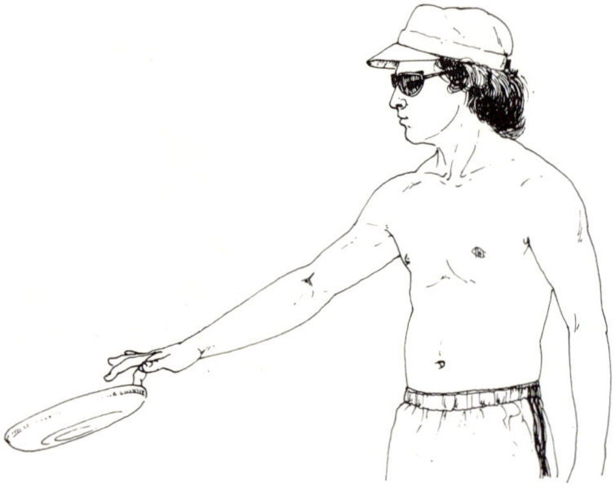

74  *Frisbee Disc Sports and Games*

For success in body skipping, allow the skip edge to strike a nearly level surface on your body rather than you trying to strike the disc.

Setting a twirl up into a delay requires a precise release of the twirl.

The totem pole, a four-player co-op move.

yond imagination a year ago. Attitude-change techniques, delay control and the turnover, among others, have provided the means for almost complete command of the disc. The old fantasy of a one-propulsion routine is now a reality.

With the wealth of techniques at a player's disposal, freestyle is reaching a new plateau. An interpretative style will become dominant in top play; that is, emphasis will be on how you do what you do. Routines will not necessarily be choreographed, but they will be better designed to reflect a particular mood or perspective of play. And routines will be more closely related to the accompanying music.

Freestyle has always held audiences enthralled. With the emergence of highly polished players, freestyle will begin to attract sophisticated audiences as do skating and gymnastics. Currently, many of the more subtle moves are wasted on audiences who have no appreciation for the difficulty involved. Television exposure with informative commentary could do much to increase the public's enjoyment of this potent new sport.

**Hitting downward on the roll shoulder produces positive attitude. The move is known as a MAC (for midair attitude control).**

**Tunnels can be very gracefully done. (Photo courtesy of Dan Poynter from *The Frisbee Player's Handbook*.)**

# 6. Guts

Guts-like games were among the very first to have written rules for disc play; for example, the famous Sky Pie package of 1949 outlined a game in which players stood 45 feet apart and scored their points exactly as in Guts. Later, the Mystery Y carried similar rules on its underside. The first documented use of the term "Guts" was in the description of a match played in 1954 at Dartmouth. That game was played with cookie tins!

The International Frisbee Tournament must be credited with the birth and development of the modern game. That event, which started in 1958 as a family picnic, is still held during the Fourth of July holidays every year in Upper Peninsula Michigan, and Guts is the main attraction. In 1968 word of the event filtered to the "outside" world—players from California attended and won. Serious enthusiasm for the game followed, and playing skills began improving dramatically.

Rules of play varied each year and were decided at the players' meeting at each IFT. The present rules were adopted by the IFA Guts Players Committee in 1975, and that committee is charged with maintaining the rules of the game.

PLAY

As with most disc games, the essence of Guts is throw and catch. But at what velocities! In top-flight games, the more interesting aspect is the battle of wits and wills. Turning will into action requires certain skills:

**Snagging an eighty-mile-an-hour throw is an exhilarating experience.**

*Throwing.* Speed, flight movement, and control are the basic considerations. Top players fire the disc at more than eighty miles an hour, but speed means nothing if you can't throw consistent strikes. Moreover, the better catchers can handle anything you throw right at them. If you don't force them to reach high or low into the creases between them and their fellow players, you won't do much scoring. That's what control is all about, and you can believe it is more critical than speed.

Flight movement refers to the tendency of some flights to dip or roll over. Straight, level flights are child's play, no matter how well placed. A disc that is corkscrewing around presents problems. Remember though, the disc cannot turn beyond vertical as it crosses the goal line.

Most players select one delivery. Others use two or three, varying them for specific situations or for

**The receiving team crouches waiting for the arrival of the disc. Getting up on the toes allows the receiving players to move quickly after a deflected disc.**

**Touching up to get proper spacing before the throw comes.**

**This is why they call it Guts. The impact of a hard throw can buckle the disc.**

# SKY-PIE - The Flying Disc Games

### THROWING—

The Sky-Pie can be thrown from sidearm or backhand delivery. For best results throw so it leaves your hand level, no tilt to either side. Good players learn both deliveries. After mastering the low level throws, curves by tilting will come natural.

### BOOMERANGING—

Throw into the Wind. The harder you throw the better it boomerangs. The harder the wind, the less incline necessary to bring it back to you. A 45 degree incline is necessary on a still day.

### GAMES—

There are numerous games played with Sky-Pie: in the yard, on the sidewalk, in the park or on tennis courts. While you no doubt will devise several to best suit your own needs, here are several that have already been developed and are being played.

### SKY-PIE—

(regulation) Each player has a court 5 ft. square and courts are 45 ft. apart. Players must be in their court to throw but can run out of their courts to make a catch. A "good" throw is one that can be reached without stepping out of the box and that is knee high when it reaches the catcher, it also must be not more than 20 degrees off level. Vertical throws are barred. Each bad throw counts one point, each miss of a good throw counts one point. A catch of a bad throw counts two points. The Pie must be caught with the foil without the aid of the free hand. There are 25 points to a game. If tie at 24, deuce is called and two consecutive points must be obtained to win. Curves, feints and change of pace are permissible. Note: where no court is marked off, one step in any direction can easily act as your court. This game is much fun for two players. Skill, equal to playing tennis or like games can be developed.

### TEAM SKY-PIE—

(regulation) Each player has his own foil and one SKY-PIE is used for each team of two players and any amount of teams can play. Each player has a throwing court 5 ft. square and team mates are separated by a distance of 45 ft. A player must be in his court to throw but can run anywhere to make his catch. Each catch counts one point. The team that makes 25 catches first wins. Each team must shout their score as each point is made. In this game the SKY-PIE is thrown back and forth between team partners as rapidly and as accurate as your skill will allow. Throw so they are easy for your partner to catch. Good players use one hand for holding the foil and the other for throwing. This is a most exciting game, as both speed and skill are necessary to win.

### GOAL SKY-PIE—

This game is played like Kick-Ball, using the Sky-Pie instead of a foot-ball. The game is started by one team throwing from the 40 yd. line. It is thrown so it is least likely to be caught, for when caught the catcher gets three steps forward before he throws it back. The object of the game is to throw the Pie over the other team's goal line, and avoid their catching it. The Pie is thrown back from the first point it touches ground. Change defending goals after each goal scored. Throw hard, low and to the least expected locations. Avoid incline throws, because it will boomerang and lose ground for your team. Throws that go out of bounds are called back at point where it went out. The foils are not used in this game.

### How Science Found the Secret of Balancing the Disc

The inventor, as a boy, like all boys, had tried to throw discs or "sailors" as they were called. He found then that if thrown so they rotated counterclockwise they would always dive to the right and when thrown clockwise they would always dive to the left. They just never would make a stable, steady flight. When all this FLYING DISC furor broke, with the papers full of it, he made himself a few discs and again verified how inherently unstable a disc was. In the meantime he had studied aerodynamics, so now with some hard thought he was able to figure out why a disc would, as it always should, make a dive instead of a long steady flight. This was now so clear and proof so convincing that he was writing an article on "The FOLLY of FLYING DISCS", when he first got an idea on how this inherent unstability might be overcome. After much work and many disappointments he was able to make a disc so stable that it no longer would make an arc! Because of this, if thrown with an incline it actually stops in midair at the end of its upward flight, only to come riding down this incline back to the thrower. BOOMERANG! And so the disc, the most unstable of all flying things, had become the most stable.

### HALL MFG. CO., Los Angeles
#### DISTRIBUTED BY
### HAMMATT & SONS

Patent Pending      Copyright 1949

(Sky Pie package liner courtesy of John Kirkland.)

endurance in long tournaments. Some of these multiple-delivery throwers try to disguise what their throw will be with all manner of backward run-ups and twisting deliveries. Such excessive trickery usually gives up more in accuracy and power than is gained in deception.

The thumber is the most popular shot in modern play. Its advantages are
- the thrower faces the target at delivery
- a hard throw produces a pronounced dipping movement
- a flight very nearly vertical is produced with a natural delivery.

**Backhands can be delivered with a whiplike motion that makes it hard for the receiving team to guess ahead of time where it is headed.**

**Thumbers can really hum. Plus, they have a tendency to pop down toward the ground that makes them really hard to snag.**

**Handling bobbles is not as easy as it looks. Many Guts teams practice this skill by flipping butterfly tosses up in their midst.**

**Joe Youngman is widely considered to have the best backhand in the game.**

**The thumber is the premier Guts throw.**

Even though thumbers can't compare with sidearms in distance competition, they seem to travel with, if anything, more velocity on the Guts court. They also possess more spin than sidearmed discs do, producing a stronger tendency for the disc to pop out of a catcher's hand.

The backhand is a throw many people adopt for no better reason than that they are already comfortable with it. It does lend itself to control. It can be well concealed and "whipped" at the opponents before they can read the intended line of flight. And it can be delivered in a wide range of angles—from nearly vertical skip curve to nearly vertical roll curve—with little modification of the run-up or release.

Hook thumbers are prized for their barrel-roll flight, and sidearms can be made to hum. Spend some time with each of these throws to determine which is the one for you.

*Catching.* One of the most challenging aspects of Guts for the individual player is that you must receive as well as give. Many big throwers never do well at Guts because their catching game is weak. If they are tried severely, their throwing usually tires and the match is lost. Teams should try to protect their weak catchers by placing them between strong hands or on the end of the line. Good throwers will still hit them.

Consistent catching demands superb hand-eye coordination, fierce concentration, and long experience

## OFFICIAL RULES OF GUTS

### THE GAME

Guts is a disc sport involving two teams of one to five persons each. The recommended number of players per team is five outdoors and four indoors or for small tournaments.

Each team lines up fingertip to fingertip along parallel goal lines fourteen meters apart (15 yards, 11 inches).

The object of the game is to deliver a good throw in such a manner that the receiving team cannot make a clean catch.

Teams should switch ends of the court at 11-point (cumulative) intervals.

To begin the game, one captain flips the disc and the other captain calls top or bottom. The winner of the flip has the choice of first throw or which side of the field to defend.

### SCORING

A good throw not resulting in a clean catch scores one point for the throwing team.

A good throw resulting in a clean catch scores no point.

A bad throw scores a point for the receiving team.

Each game is played to a minimum of twenty-one points.

A team must have a two-point lead to win.

### THROWING

A catch requires that the catcher attempt the next throw.

A good throw touched, but not caught, requires the next throw be made by the player who first touched it.

A good throw, not touched, permits any player on the receiving team to attempt the next throw.

A good throw must satisfy all the following requirements:
Traverses the fourteen-meter court without touching the ground and is within the receiving team's optimum effort.
Crosses or hits the goal line topside up at an angle of less than ninety degrees to the ground.
Must be delivered from behind or on the 14-meter foul line (stepping completely over the line before or during the release constitutes a foot fault).
Is not bent intentionally to alter the true flight.

The teammates of the thrower must stand where they will not inhibit the vision on the receiving team.

The throwing team must place a player at the end of the throwing line to call foot faults as they occur.

### OPTIMUM EFFORT

Optimum effort is the extension of the hands and arms by the player on the receiving team nearest the disc as it crosses the goal line.

Optimum effort does not require that the player leave the ground to reach the throw.

If a receiving player jumps, a throw by or below the required outstretched hand is good.

## CATCHING

A clean catch must satisfy all the following requirements:
Be held in one hand long enough to establish complete control.
Not be touched by any two parts of a player's body at any one time.
Not touch the ground.

All players on the receiving team must toe the goal line until the throw is released.

## JUDGING

The players are the judges.

In general, the thrower should judge the throw and the catcher should judge the catch.

In the event of a dispute, team captains only will meet at center court to discuss and resolve it.

If the dispute cannot be resolved, the throw attempt will be repeated.

Additional judges may be used if they are invited by the Guts tournament director and the captain of one of the teams playing the game; or by both team captains; or all three parties.

## MISCELLANY

The Pro model Frisbee® is the disc to be used for Guts.

Foot Faults—A foot fault on the throw constitutes a point for the receiving team.

Substitutions may be made at every eleven-point switch with no restriction on players returning to play.

Gloves may be worn. They should be unpadded (not to exceed one thickness of leather over the palm).

The disc may be touched by more than one player at a time provided no single player touches it with two parts of the body at one time.

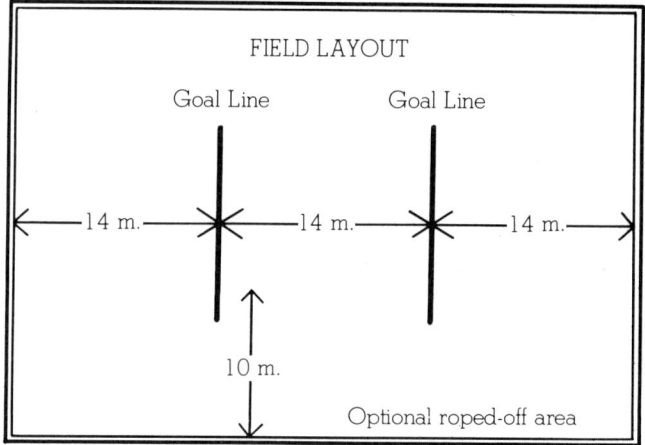

## SUGGESTIONS

Playing area—Surface should be essentially level and smooth. If a grass surface is used it should be closely trimmed. Spectators should not be allowed within the playing area which should be demarcated by lines or rope in heavy crowd situations.

A rope secured in place on each goal line accomplishes three things. First, it provides a three-dimensional line, making foot faults psychologically and physically more obvious. Second, low throws are more obvious because the disc makes an unusual bounce and sound as it strikes the rope. Third, the rope won't wear away or become any less sharp as the field becomes worn. The rope, of course must be secured; hooked wires are suggested on grass, and tape on hard sufaces.

**One that got away.**

**Scooping one off the ground.**

**Scrambling after a deflection.**

**Another one that got away.**

in the trenches. Since the disc arrives in a third of a second, reaction to it must be spontaneous. Old pros will often attempt catches with upward motions of their hand in order to increase the likelihood the disc will travel upward if the catch is muffed. The same motive should find players trying to make initial contact at the roll shoulder (where possible deflection or MAC might save a blown catch) except on very steep skip angles, but this has not been the case so far.

The recovery of missed catches is an art in itself. Handling these bobbles calls for a soft touch that will keep the disc up if it again eludes the snag. Many teams practice this art by flipping butterfly tosses up among themselves. A disc caught flat on the palm is legal, and that often happens at the end of a long bobble. (A disc lying fully on the palm but touching the wrist is not considered a trap. One lying partly on the hand and partly on the forearm is a trap.)

## STRATEGY

Probing for weaknesses is the prime throwing strategy. Close games go to the first team to find an opponent's inability to handle clock-spin roll curves coming from slightly to the right arriving on the left side just below the knee, or whatever. A good team can be relentless once having sniffed out such a weakness. And nothing is so demoralizing as watching a teammate suffer strike after strike while there is little you can do.

**The difference between an average Guts team and a great one is the ability to recover and pursue deflections.**

**No matter how far the disc sails overhead, the receiving players should make optimum effort. This requires that they straighten up and extend their arms to full reach, but they need not jump.**

Not enough players take advantage of the fact that you do not have to throw from the center of your goal line. And some players seem to think you must throw at the center of the opponents' line as well. That's where the strongest catcher usually plays!

The point is to avoid being predictable. You can tell where some players are going to throw well before they release. Better players have "loosey-goosey" deliveries that are impossible to read in advance. Vary the direction of your throws—don't fire them all straight across. But don't sail them at such an angle that the time it takes the disc to cross the court increases significantly.

Catching strategy, beyond what has already been mentioned about protecting weaker catchers, involves working out coverage patterns to insure movement to the disc if not caught on first contact; for example, a shot might produce the movement shown in the diagrams on this page. You don't have time to contemplate where to go in a third of a second, so reaction patterns should be rehearsed until they become instinctive.

Remember, every throw is a point-producing opportunity. Don't hurry. Take the time to think out where you want to mail each throw and what sort of postage you want on it. Make your throw count. There is no excuse—none—for giving up a point on a bad throw.

## DRAMA

Guts is a game of unbridled aggression, it is a game of psych-outs, it is a game of intimidation. Aggressive confidence is essential. If you stand on line hoping the throw doesn't come to you, if you don't

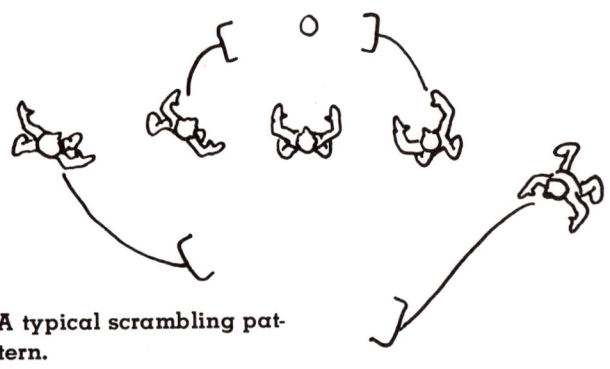

**A typical scrambling pattern.**

feel like letting out a war whoop after snagging eighty miles per hour of flying plastic, if you can't paw the ground and stare intense fury at your opponents before your throw, you probably don't belong in a Guts match.

The rhythms of the game are marvelous to behold: the steady buildup of tension once the disc has been handed to the new thrower; the taut air being shredded by the bellowing of the thrower; the whistling of the disc; and the grunts of the catchers; those who dish out must also take; all of this over and over in each match. The rhythmic cycles of the game promote ritual behavior—back pounding, hugging, hand slapping, taunting. The demeanor of a team surging into the lead usually resembles shark feeding frenzy.

You should be aware of the drama of the game

and be prepared to add to it. Think of it: How many opportunities do you get to go at someone as hard as you can? . . . and without fear of injuring them? Guts injuries are limited to broken nails and busted capillaries. Even those can be nearly eliminated with the use of gloves. As much as anything, the complete Guts player is an exuberant showman.

## FUTURE

The game has phenomenal spectator appeal, no doubt because of the drama, but also because of the simplicity of its format and strategies and because of its typically American flavor. Even first-time spectators get carried away. Guts comes across exceptionally well on television.

**Scrambling is a team effort. Every team member should be alert to the possibility of a deflection.**

Probably many more people are interested in watching Guts than in playing it. It is not an easy game to get into. It can be a bit intimidating for a new player, especially because the weak guy gets most of the action. The secret to getting into Guts is in selecting players of comparable skill levels.

Since the beauty of Guts is its simplicity, it is hard to suggest any new direction for the game to take. The only real problems are the calls on vertical and high throws. Observers may be needed, as it is a matter of perception, not integrity.

**A light touch is required to recover bobbles. The disc can be juggled any number of times so long as no one player ever touches it with more than one part of the body at one time.**

The formation of the Guts Players Association bodes well for the growth of the game; currently it is the most regional of all disc sports, concentrated as it is in the midwestern U.S. The promotion and exposure it has been receiving insure that it will gain in popularity both as a player sport and a spectator sport.

## RELATED GAMES

*Flatball.* Flatball is the brainchild of Victor Malafronte. It differs from Guts in several respects: Play is continuous, players defend a court rather than a goal line, catches may be made in any fashion, and upside-down throws are permitted.

Throws landing in or passing through the opponents' court without being touched score 3 points. Throws touched and landing inside the court score 2 points, and throws touched and landing outside the court score 1 point. No point is awarded on bad throws.

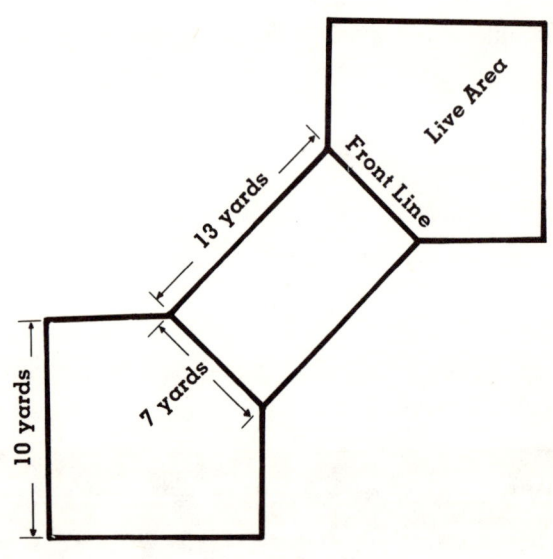

**A Flatball court.**

# 7. Ultimate

Few disc games have as definite an origin as Ultimate. In 1967, Columbia High School students in Maplewood, New Jersey, devised what has become the most overwhelmingly popular disc field game. The students, headed by Rich Denberg, Joel Silver, and Irv Kalb, started by playing the game locally, but soon dubbed themselves "CHS Varsity Frisbee" and initiated development of a high school league in northern New Jersey.

By 1972, Columbia High graduates were starting teams at the college level. The first collegiate game was a rematch of Rutgers and Princeton, the first teams to play a college football game. Rutgers won by two, just as they had 103 years earlier. Collegiate play expanded rapidly in the East with more than thirty teams playing by the 1974 season. Rutgers emerged as the powerhouse, putting together a string of 48 victories and four national titles between 1972 and 1975.

The game spread nationally, and 1977 featured the first East-West national championship. In that game, the Santa Barbara Condors upset highly favored Penn State, pride of the East.

The number of high school, college, and club teams grows dramatically larger. In fact, Ultimate scholarships have been given out. Despite the rapid spread of the game and although changes have been made over the year (the seventh edition of the rules is printed here), the game remains much as it was originally designed.

**The pull starts play. Smart teams will hang the pull up and land it near the sideline to bottle the offense up from the start.**

## PLAYING SKILLS

Ultimate could fill a book of its own on the techniques of play, but we'll have to limit this discussion to a few general considerations.

**A huddle before the throw-off gives a team a chance to work out guarding assignments and other strategic matters.**

**Lining up to receive the pull (throw-off).**

*Throwing.* Needless to say, strong throwing skills are vital. A wide range of deliveries is helpful in order to evade close coverage. Trajectory control is essential to bypass downfield defenders and tailor passes to the movement of the receiver. Wobbly, uncertain, or hanging passes are quickly punished by a good defense. Throwing under close guard is a unique Ultimate skill, one that comes slowly to some disc players. It is quite easy to become flustered with an eager defender in your face.

Passes must be sure and swift. Backhands predominate. Sidearms are valuable and so are wrist flips. Pushes get lots of use at close range. Straight, level, low, and fast is the best philosophy. Use curve throws, upside-down lobs, and other finesse throws sparingly and only when the risk is warranted.

*Catching.* Two-handed catching may make it sound as if receptions are easily made in Ultimate. Wrong! Many a talented Guts or freestyle player has dropped a two-handed pancake in the Ultimate end zone. The conditions for catching are murderous: you're moving, the disc is moving, and other people very much want to take the disc from you. Good hands are only the beginning; good concentration is crucial. Perhaps the most valuable Ultimate talent is the ability to catch in a crowd, consistently. Pulling down floaters requires a knack for positioning, timing, and leaping. Height doesn't hurt.

Theoretically, you are better off to catch with both hands around the rim of the disc than with one hand on top and one hand on the bottom (pancake). The catch is surer and you can ready your throw sooner.

*Running.* Good movement is essential for good play. No other field game requires as much constant running as Ultimate. Each player is like a wide receiver in football running an endless pass pattern. Sharp cuts and variations in running speed will help you get open. Running conditioning should be practiced both during and between seasons. Defensive movement is particularly demanding; a few faltering steps can wreck the best-laid defense.

**The margins for getting a pass off against close coverage are pretty slim.**

**An experienced passer takes defensive coverage for granted and concentrates on the downfield space.**

## TACTICAL SKILLS

All tactical considerations spring from this simple truth: When your team has the disc, everybody on your team plays offense; when their team has the disc, everybody on your team plays defense. Most of what we are about to present is not part of current play, but it is on the horizon, for the most established teams anyway. We present these ideas as food for thought.

*Offensive Qualities.* The objective of the offense is always to penetrate the defense. That is accomplished with forward passes. Everything an offense does should be done to increase their chance of completing forward passes.

Superior attacks will have the following qualities, though these may appear in myriad configurations. Throughout this section the discussion is general, and it will be up to you to apply it to your team's particular talents.

• Depth—The key to penetration is the ability to control the expanse of field in front of the disc. Receivers too far downfield are not much threat to a

**Some players rely on the push for close-range passes.**

defense; neither is an attack strung across the field. The more players in position to receive forward passes, the more pressure on the defense.

• Width—The counter to defensive solidity is width. Width spreads a defense out, opening spaces

**The sidearm is a handy quick-release throw for getting off a pass around an aggressive defender.**

for downfield passing. Width also allows the offense to shift its point of attack quickly, unbalancing the defense.

• Fluidity—Offenses that employ static formations require the defense only to keep track of the disc. Highly mobile attacks that shift positions frequently unbalance the defense and create scoring threats.

• Support—Penetration cannot take place if receivers do not get open for *productive* passes. Stay mobile and get open or help others get open. When a receiver is needed, you should be there.

*Defensive Qualities.* The objective of the defense is to get the disc. This can be accomplished, over the long run, only with a combination of unrelenting containment and opportunistic interception attempts.

The defenses that force the most turnovers will have the following qualities:

• Solidity—Choose the territory where you wish to make the defensive stand. The ability to corral offensive depth is achieved by deploying compactly and economically throughout that area and shutting down productive passing lanes.

• Articulation—There are no doubts about guarding assignments or other defensive duties. The more articulate a defense, the better it can respond to novelty.

• Balance—A properly set-up defense will be able to apply numerical superiority to any point of attack.

• Self-control—Players who can be lured out of position by offensive tricks or who overcommit when guarding or going for the disc can be the downfall of an otherwise sound defense.

• Playmaking—If the offense doesn't give you the disc back, you have to take it. A wise team knows when to gamble for the disc and to apply bold tactics. Obviously, there is a fine line between playmaking and loss of self-control.

**Catching under close guarding demands the utmost in concentration.**

*Offensive Tactics.* It has been said that the best Ultimate teams will be made up of soccer players who have been taught how to throw a Frisbee disc. It is true that many teams not lacking in disc-handling skills remain mediocre for lack of intelligent positioning play. Learning to play the field properly takes much longer than learning to pass the disc.

After a turnover or pull (throw-off), offenses can respond with two basic strategies: counterattack or slow buildup. Counterattack—quick penetration—offers the most possibilities and is most effective when the opposing team was fully committed to their at-

**Catches are seldom simple. Ultimate owes much of its spectator appeal to the fantastic catches that are often made.**

tack at the time they gave up the disc. Rapid downfield movement and passing do the trick. A slow buildup should only be used to kill time, to gain time for regrouping, or to exasperate a defense. A slow buildup is characterized by lots of back-and-forth crossfield passing.

On a turnover, remember, you do not have to pick up the disc just because you are closest to it. Very likely, you will want to sprint downfield, letting a teammate behind you put the disc in play. Other basic attack tactics that can be employed by teams at all levels of experience are to avoid bunching up when going downfield, and likewise, to avoid stringing out (try to form triangles with nearby teammates). Receivers should run toward the goal at angles so that they present better targets and, at the same time, should avoid putting more than one defender between themselves and the disc, except of course for brief intervals when crossing to a better position. Use give-and-go passes to work the disc quickly downfield. Use crossfield passes only when they set up forward passes, or as an out when severely pressured by a guarder, or when probing for defensive weaknesses near the goal line. Threaten goals to put pressure on the defense. Help set up passing lanes by luring defenders out the of the way (known as clear-and-fill: you clear a space, a less well-guarded teammate fills to receive the pass). Because Ultimate players cannot run the disc, receivers need to advance quickly whenever a forward pass is completed. Finally, communicate with your teammates.

**Pivoting is an art every Ultimate player needs to learn in order to get passes away around close coverage.**

Near the goal line, continuous, purposeful movement is more important than ever. Receivers should be aware not only of their pass-receiving potential at the moment, but also of how to get or stay open in the event a crossfield pass changes the point of attack.

Experienced teams can employ somewhat more advanced tactics. Audible play calling could get a bogged-down counterattack on track again. Such plays at this time will probably be no more intricate than providing coded directions to a couple of receivers to break into certain pass patterns. They could easily develop into multi-stage attack plans in the not-too-distant future. Another ploy is to blitz unguarded rear players downfield on cue.

Imagine this situation: A teammate sends a short push pass to you, then streaks downfield. You try to throw a backhand back to the center of the field, but can find no one open. Suddenly, the teammate who passed to you squares out toward the sideline and gets open for a moment, but you are on the wrong side of the player guarding you to get off a pass. It would have been much better if your teammate had given you a hand signal after the pass that said, "In fifteen yards, I'll square out." Then you could have whirled on your defender and delivered a sidearm back to your teammate just as he or she broke free.

Such plays are called patterned runs. They are potent offensive weapons and should be in every team's attack arsenal. Worked out in a little more detail, patterned runs can be used to set up killer passes, long forward passes into the heart of a defense that score or threaten to set up a score immediately.

The killer pass brings up the subject of its longer cousin—the bomb, the forty or sixty meter pass. First, there is little reason to try a bomb that won't score: The receiver will have to wait for teammates to advance upfield; meanwhile, the defense can get built up. Second, many players don't realize how much a disc, particularly a 165-G, slows down over that range. A throw of fifty meters takes more than four seconds to arrive. That's longer than the hang time of most punts in football. Every player within 25 meters of the target will have time to get there. Use the bomb if you can lead it right, use it to keep the defense honest, and go for a score when you do use it. Don't use it much.

*Defensive Tactics.* Debate has raged since schoolyard days at Columbia High over which is better, the zone defense or the person-on-person defense. Talented teams have won with the zone, but then talented teams could be expected to win frequently anyway. The fact is, the zone derives its popularity from the freelance spirit of most Frisbee disc players. The person-on-person defense requires more discipline, but it is more effective.

The advantage the person-on-person offers a team that hasn't played together much is its articulateness; that is, you cover the opposing player assigned to you and that is your only defensive duty. Its biggest advantage, though, is that it is utterly demoralizing to the opposition, largely because it dampens their freelance spirit. (Receivers like to feel open.) Only a really savvy team can exploit its disadvantages. It can be made to give up balance (if one attacker gets free long enough to give numerical superiority to the point of attack, much damage can be done before the defense recovers). It yields the initiative (defen-

**This is the usual scene when the disc hangs up. Nearly everyone on the field has time to converge on it. Being able to catch in crowds like this requires sharp positioning, good leaping ability, and timing.**

Ultimate 97

Using the legs is an effective guarding technique, but the defender must be careful to keep his weight over his foot so he can recover if the passer pivots on him.

Once a defender lunges to block a disc, the passer has a chance to pivot and get off a clear shot.

There are ways to improve on it if a team is willing to put in the necessary practice time. A few simple concepts will help mark the way to the defense of the future:

Guarding—covering a potential receiver skintight (a new term needs to be coined for covering a thrower).

Patrolling—covering receivers just tightly enough to play for an interception, or to get right on them if they get a pass.

Foraging—very opportunistic defensive play with the purpose of keeping the defensive balance shifted to the point of attack.

Least-threatened—defenders covering attackers who aren't in position to receive a productive pass.

The defense of the future will maintain a shifting mixture of the three types of defensive play, say two patrollers up front challenging the throwers and other rear attackers, four guarders covering the most likely receivers, and a forager following the flow of play to double-team prime receivers, play for the interception, pick up a blitz, or fill in for a defender who slips down.

In general, every receiver within about twenty yards of the disc must be closely guarded. As the receiver gets farther from the disc, the defender can more afford to patrol—keeping a balance between playmaking and self-control, however. A fleet player with a knack for making interceptions should do most of the foraging, but even the forager will frequently be required to do close guarding. If you will

ders' moves are dictated by attackers' moves). And it can be forced to give up depth (dangerous spaces can be opened in the middle of a defense when the receivers spread out more than usual).

**Every Ultimate player's dream: alone in the end zone under a floater.**

simple articulation will be more important to effectiveness than flexibility.

The response of a defense to loss of the disc or to a killer pass should be harass-and-delay. The defenders nearest the disc should put maximum pressure on the thrower and nearest receivers until the less-threatened defenders have a chance to fall back and set up. Crossfield passing lanes may be left open if necessary, but downfield lanes should be closed by stacking defenders in them as thickly as possible. Particularly if the disc is lost in the opponent's half of the field, the defense may prefer to ap-

look back at the list of defensive qualities, you will see that a defense built on these concepts promotes all of those qualities.

The concept of least-threatened is important for defensive articulation. A defender should stick with whomever she or he is covering until reaching a reasonably least-threatened position. Then it is possible to switch assignments safely with a nearby teammate, if desired.

Established teams should try to work out flexible defenses along those lines. A team that does not intend to play together for many games, however, should stick with straight person-on-person defense or with formation defenses, (such as 2-3-2) because

**The idea behind guarding the passer is not to try to knock down any pass, but to take away the most productive passing lanes. That usually means shading toward the middle of the field to allow passes only to the rear or toward the sideline.**

ply total pressure to gamble on getting the disc right back, rather than to fall back for a defensive buildup.

The most important ingredient for any defense is to use extensive visual and oral communication. Players should call out their assignments (I'll take 41); should alert teammates (Possible blitz on you, Rachel); should compliment each other (Way to stick on him, Ted); and should announce new play developments (They're going back across field).

## FUTURE

Ultimate is a paradox. It is at once the most satisfactory and least satisfactory disc sport: Most satisfactory because of its broad appeal and ability to generate enthusiasm, because of its complex strategies within a very simple framework, and because of its potential to become the first really major disc sport; and least satisfactory mainly because it treats the disc as a mere token that distinguishes offense

**Pressing the offense is a good defensive tactic when the offense is deep in its end of the field. Turnovers can be turned into goals before a team can regroup to defend.**

# OFFICIAL RULES OF ULTIMATE

Ultimate is a fast-moving, competitive, non-contact sport played by two seven-person teams. The sport has a great amount of freedom and informality implicit in the rules. Primary among these is the spirit of sportsmanship which enables the honor system to be effective.

Ultimate has traditionally been considered an alternative athletic activity. Highly competitive play is encouraged but never at the expense of the bond of mutual respect between players of the basic joy of play. Protection of these vital elements eliminates some type of "sport" behavior from the Ultimate field. Such actions as taunting of opposition players, dangerous aggression, intentional fouling or other "win at all costs" behaviors are fouls against the spirit of the game and should be discouraged by all players.

The object of Ultimate is to gain points by scoring goals. The disc may only be passed, and a goal is scored when a player successfully passes the disc to a teammate in the end zone which that team is attacking. The team with the most points at the end of the game is declared the winner.

## EQUIPMENT

The Wham-O 165-G is the official disc to be used in tournament play. Individual players may wear almost any aids they wish, including hats, helmets or gloves as long as they do not endanger the safety of any other player. For example, shoes with cleats are permissible but ones with sharp spikes are not. No player may carry any sort of stick, bat, or racket.

## PLAYING FIELD

The playing field may have any surface whatsoever including grass, asphalt, sand, snow, or the wood of a gymnasium floor. The main playing field for the official Ultimate game is 60 yards long and 40 yards wide. Both end zones are 40 yards wide and 30 yards deep. Optional, metric field dimensions are 55 meters long and 35 meters wide with end zones 35 meters wide and 25 meters deep.

## OUT OF BOUNDS

If a pass is completed outside the lateral boundary, it is considered incomplete and the defensive team gains possession of the disc. In order to be considered in-bounds, a player must land with both feet inside the lateral boundary line (the side line itself is out-of-bounds). Should the disc land outside the lateral boundary, it is returned to play on the main playing field at the point where the disc went out of bounds. The player throwing the disc in-bounds must have his/her pivot foot on the line.

## OFFICIALS

A referee or referees may officiate, and their decision must be final. If no referee is used, the two teams play on an honor system. Each team should provide one person to keep time and score.

## TIME

A game of Ultimate lasts for 48 minutes of playing time, divided into two 24-minute halves. Halftime lasts for ten minutes. The clock starts after every throw-off when the receiving team touches the disc. The clock stops after every goal, at the end of each period of play, for time-outs, injuries, fouls and when the disc goes out-of-bounds. The clock starts when the disc is thrown in-bounds or when both teams are ready to resume, and play continues at the location of the disc when the play stopped.

Each team is permitted three time-outs per half and one per

overtime period, each lasting two minutes. Time-out may be called by either team after a goal and before the ensuing throw-off. A team must be in possession of the disc in order to call a time-out during play.

In the event of a tie at the end of regulation time, there will be an overtime period lasting five minutes. The captains flip a coin to determine which team will throw-off. If there is no winner at the end of this period, overtimes are continued until the tie is broken at the end of one period.

## THROW-OFF

Play begins with the throw-off. The captains of the two teams flip a coin to determine which team will throw or receive, or choice of goal. The teams shall alternate throw-offs at the beginning of each period. All players must be on or behind their own goal line until the disc is released. Both teams must stand on their own goal line without changing relative position.

A player on the goal line throws the disc toward the other team. As soon as the disc is released, all players may cross the goal lines. No player on the throwing team may touch the disc in the air before it is touched by a member of the receiving team.

The receiving team may catch the disc or allow it to fall untouched to the ground. If a member of the receiving team successfully catches the throw-off, that player has possession at that point. If the receiving team touches the disc and fails to catch it, the team which threw off gains possession of the disc where it is stopped. If the disc is allowed to fall untouched to the ground, the receiving team has possession where it is stopped.

If the disc goes out-of-bounds (endline and/or sideline), the receiving team makes the immediate decision of (1) having the disc thrown off again, (2) gaining possession at the point the disc went out-of-bounds, or (3) if the disc goes out-of-bounds after crossing the goal line, the receiving team may elect to take possession on the goal line at the nearest corner.

Each time a goal is scored, the teams switch direction of their attack, and the team which scored throws-off on the signal of the receiving team.

## END ZONES

Any time a team gains possession in the end zone which they are defending, the player immediately chooses to resume play where the disc is stopped, or at the goal line. A player may carry the disc up to the goal line provided that he/she approaches it perpendicularly. The player may not pass the disc during the approach to the goal line. If a team gains possession in the end zone which it is attacking, the disc is *carried* perpendicularly to the goal line and then play resumes immediately from the goal line.

## THE PLAY

The team which has possession of the disc must attempt to move the disc into position so that they may score a goal. A player may propel the disc in any way he/she wishes. The disc may never be handed from player to player. In order for the disc to go from one player to another, it must at some time be in the air.

*No player may walk, run or take steps while in possession of the disc.* The momentum of the receiver, however, must be taken into consideration. Should a player take steps obviously not required to stop, a foul is called. The player in possession may pivot on one foot, as in basketball. The thrower may not change the pivot foot. If the thrower changes the pivot foot, a foul is called.

The defensive team gains possession whenever the offensive team's pass is incomplete, intercepted, knocked down, or goes out-of-bounds. A rolling or sliding disc may be stopped by any player, but may not be advanced in any direction. After the disc is stopped, no defensive player may touch it. Possession is gained at the point where the disc is stopped. Any member of the team gaining possession of the disc may throw it.

A player may catch his/her own throw only if the disc has been touched by another player during its flight. Bobbling to gain control is permitted, but tipping to oneself is not allowed.

## FOULS

A throwing foul is called only by the player fouled. Any physical contact during the throw is a foul against the defender. The thrower may not push the player defending. Contact occurring during the follow-through (after release of the disc) is not sufficient grounds for a foul. If the pass is completed, the foul is automatically declined and play proceeds without stopping.

Players must play the disc, not the opponent. That is, they may not position themselves or move for the purpose of impeding other players. To do so is a foul. In playing the disc, players must respect the established positions of others. Low momentum contact during and after the catching attempt is often unavoidable and is not a foul. Violent impact with legitimately positioned opponents constitues harmful endangerment, is a foul, and must be strictly avoided.

A stalling violation occurs when the player guarding the thrower calls out "stalling" and counts aloud 15 seconds. If the disc has not been released at the end of the count, it is turned over to the defense at that point.

## CALLING A FOUL

The player who is fouled calls "foul," play stops and the player gains possession at the point of the infraction. For a momentum or pivoting foul, play stops, a "check" of the disc occurs, but possession is retained by the thrower. Play continues when both teams are ready (see clarifying statements). Should a foul occur in the end zone, possession is gained at the goal line.

## SCORING

A goal is scored when an offensive player lands in bounds with any part of both feet in the end zone after receiving a pass from a teammate. The goal line is not considered part of the endzone. A player in possession may not score by running into the end zone. The team that scores receives one point.

Only *one* player may guard the person in possession of the disc. The disc may not be wrenched from the grasp of an opposing player or knocked from his/her hand. If the disc is dropped by the thrower without interference by a defender, a turnover results. If the disc is simultaneously caught, offense retains possession.

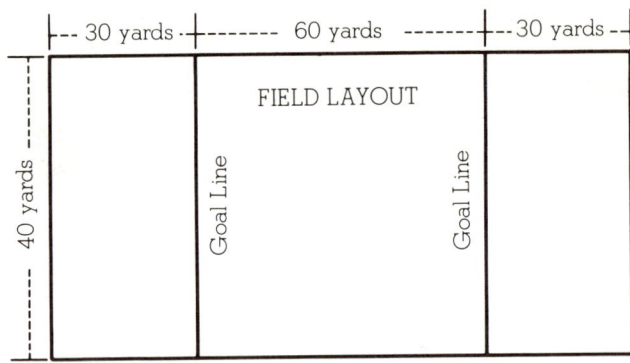

## SUBSTITUTIONS

Substitutions can be made only (1) after a goal and before the ensuing throw-off, (2) to replace an injured player, or (3) after periods of play. Substitutions cannot be made during a timeout.

## CLARIFYING STATEMENTS

There are no scrimmage lines or offsides in Ultimate. The disc may be passed in any direction—forward, to the sides, or backwards. The term "when both teams are ready" implies that a defensive player will check (hold) the disc until the defensive team is ready, and then hand the disc to the thrower, thus restarting the clock. It should be common practice that the offensive team finds a position then remains stationary until the disc is given to the thrower.

The disc may fly out of bounds and return to the playing field, but the defense may attempt to knock the disc down when the disc is out of bounds.

## VARIATIONS

Before the opening throw-off, the captains of the teams may agree on any additional ground rules necessary. The number of players, size of field, model of disc, and length of game can be adapted.

---

from defense and marks the progress of play. Such a view fails to conceive of the disc as an energy object, the way the other disc sports do to varying degrees. Many players would like to see discwork incorporated as dribbling; that is, players would be allowed to advance the disc by brushing, tipping, or delaying. This has worked with good results in Dynamo Disc (described below) and is probably just around the corner in Ultimate.

Voices have been raised against other features of the game. Why have static rectangular fields? Why not ovals, for instance? Why not have other forms of scoring (a two-point "hot spot" is often suggested) to increase the strategic dimensions of the game? There is not much point in worrying about such matters. The game will go where it goes. Remember, the forward pass didn't come around in football for more than forty years.

Ultimate generates immediate spectator interest. Play is active. Strategy is both obvious and complex. Scoring is frequent. And the flight of the disc is easily followed. Very probably, we will be seeing semi-pro league play within a couple of years.

Ultimate offers something that stands to revolutionize attitudes toward sport, thanks to the foresight of its innovators. Being aware of its potential for wide acceptance, they developed a very aggressive defense of its "integrity" as both a game and an attitude. The "spirit of the game" has been a vital part of Ultimate play and relates in a central way to its future. Can what was originally a local understanding of sportsmanship and mutual respect be transferred to hundreds of playing fields across the world?

The answer depends on how the game is presented. Essentially, it is no more prone to generate friendly play than is any other field game unless it is actively promoted in that way.

Players agree on certain limits of play, and to exceed those limits has no purpose in the game. Officials may become a reality in the role of observers to help resolve perceptual disputes, but the moral burden for legal play rightfully belongs on the player. With careful socialization of new players and strong peer pressure on the field, the "spirit" will not only continue, it may antiquate officiating in other sports.

We hope you'll get into the "spirit" of Ultimate and help others get into it. When you play Ultimate, play hard and play friendly.

RELATED GAMES

Frisbee disc play has spawned several field games. The Frisbee Game was a sanctioned event in the 1974 World Frisbee disc Championships. It was a rather complex game featuring goal cages and Guts throws. The IFA hoped to popularize it, but it died. Goal Line is another such game that is nowhere to be found today. Both of these games are well described in Stancil Johnson's book *Frisbee*, and the interested researcher is advised to look there.

Disc play can be adapted to fit the requirements of any number of players, any shape of field, any length of time, and any type of strategy. For instance, imagine a goal circle eight yards in diameter surrounded by a circle fifty or sixty yards in diameter. The object is to score by passing to a player in the goal circle, but no player is allowed to stay inside the circle more than four seconds. You can come up with countless variations, and, who knows,

like the students at Columbia High, you may come up with the game of the future.

There are two other field sports that are currently played. Whizbo is the invention of Jan Sobel and is popular in junior high programs where football-oriented youngsters take readily to scrimmage-line strategy. Dynamo Disc involves shots into a goal net as in hockey, lacrosse, and soccer. Its originators, Phil Cotroneo and Steve Blinn, have made it quite popular in the Bay Area, where the Hayward Flashers and Oakland Streakers are the big rivals for supremacy.

**Action around the arch line in Dynamo Disc, looking for a good shot at the goal.**

*Dynamo Disc.* A point is scored when the disc is thrown, skipped, or deflected into the net. The disc may be advanced by passing *or* dribbling (brushing, tipping, delaying, or short tosses to oneself). Offensive drops are called downs. On the third down of a given possession, the disc goes over to the other team. Turnovers also occur on interceptions and out-of-bounds throws. An arch area surrounds the goal net, and only one player from each team is allowed inside. The offensive player inside the arch area may score only by deflecting teammates' throws into the net.

*Whizbo.* Each team has three downs per possession to score or make another first down by crossing midfield. The field may be any convenient size and is arranged like a football field. Each down begins when the whizard (quarterback) picks up the disc,

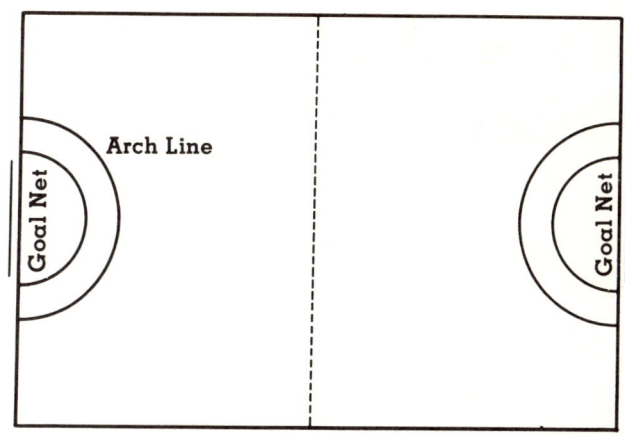

**A Dynamo Disc field**

and play proceeds with running and passing until a defender tags the player with the disc, or a pass goes incomplete. However, the whizard's first pass must be complete beyond the line of scrimmage. Passes into the end zone score 7, as do brushes, delays, or tips run into the end zone. Regular runs into the end zone score 5. Whiz-goals (similar to a field goal) score 3. A returnbo (MTA throw) is allowed for point-after attempts and fouls and scores 1 point for every two seconds of flight.

More information on these and other disc games can be obtained by contacting the IFA, Box 970, San Gabriel, California 91776.

**The goalie's job in Dynamo Disc is a demanding one.**

# Appendix I
# Other Disc Games

Hundreds and hundreds of games have been played with discs. Some are straight copies of ball games; others are uniquely disc oriented. Some can be played by anyone; some require advanced disc skills. We present a representative selection here. Because most of these games exist in many variations in different parts of the country and because they can be easily modified to make them easy or challenging to suit player skills, we present only the essentials. You can make up the particular rules.

## MOBILE ACCURACY

Tom Bodá devised this excellent game for young players and advanced players alike. It is very similar to call-your-hole golf except that the throw of a target disc determines the objective. After the target disc is thrown, each of the three to five players throws at the target in turn. After that round, each player throws another disc, this time in reverse order (last thrower first, first thrower last). The disc closest to the target is worth one point. A disc touching the target disc is worth two. Winner of each set throws the target disc, or each player may throw the target disc in turn. The first player to eleven wins.

## SPEEDFLOW

This is a great game for developing freestyle skills while concentrating on consistent performance. Each pair of players attempts to make as many catches in a given time period (usually one minute) as possible. Trick catches count double. Trailing-edge catches work well because they allow a quick rethrow. In the absence of a stopwatch, all pairs can play at once, and the first pair to reach a certain number of points wins.

## F-R-I-S-B-E-E

Played like the basketball shooting game H-O-R-S-E, using any type of golf hole or target. Players first establish an order of play. The first player attempts any type of shot. If it is successful, the next player must throw the same shot from the same place. Each hit requires the next player to take the throw from the same spot until a player misses. The player who missed gets a letter, F, R, and so on, for each player who had made the shot. The player following the one to miss is free to choose a new shot. If all players make the shot the first player may choose again, but if all players make the leader's shot twice in a row, the leader gets assigned a letter. Players who get assigned all seven letters are out.

## DISCATHON

Here's a game that can't be beat for field days or picnics. Mark off a winding course of two or three hundred yards. Several players at once race by throwing their disc (each disc should be initialed or of different colors) and running after it for the next throw. First player to throw through a Hula Hoop at the finish line wins. No short cuts!

**Short tosses are the way to improve your dog's catching style and warm her up for longer throws.**

## BOWLBEE

Bowlbee develops ground-shot skills, both rollers and gym floor curves. A target (or targets) that can be knocked down is used, and players take turns trying to topple it. In another version, a target disc is thrown on the ground or in the air, and the game is played like Mobile Accuracy using only ground throws. This version is best when there are several ground obstacles.

## CALL-SHOT

There's no better game for developing throwing variety and approach-shot skills. Each player names several conditions for a proposed throw, such as over that hedge, skip under the limb, and land on the sidewalk. Players then agree how many points the throw is worth if made, and the throw is taken.

## CO-OP FLOW

This is speedflow for advanced players. Emphasis is on consistency. Two or more co-oping pairs or trios can play. A point is scored for a team once each of the players has tricked the disc at least once. From then on, a point is scored for each player who performs a successful trick. In the advanced version, the points don't count unless a trick catch is made to end the co-op. Instructors will find this a helpful way to teach co-oping skills. See Maxi-Op.

## KEEPAWAY

Played like all monkey-in-the-middle games except that in this case the monkey may be armed with a disc to knock down the other players' throws.

## MINI GAMES

Almost every disc game or sport can be played with a Mini disc. Guts and freestyle are especially fun with a Mini. Golf can be played indoors with a Mini. MTA and TRC take on new dimensions, and Mini discs can be thrown in several novel ways. It's always a good idea to have a dozen or so Minis on hand for rainy days.

## THROW, SPLASH & DROWN

An identical game to TRC except straight into ocean surf. Best played when feeling crazy.

## DIVING BOARD FREESTYLE

Teams of two must complete a series of trick catches. Throws are made from the end of the pool across from the diving board and the catcher must be off the board for the catch to count. To complete a required trick, each team member must do the trick on a throw from their partner. Teams come up to the board in rotation and must stay on one trick until both players complete it. Suggested order: behind the back, between the legs (front), behind the head, between the legs (back), knee trap, blind.

First team done wins. First team to drown loses.

## THE BIG TUNNEL

How many people can you get to hold their hands together (two-person hoops)? Now, can you throw through them to a trick catch at the other end?

## SKIP DISC

A number of court games have been devised around skipping the disc. Generally, there are two foul lines sixty to eighty feet apart with a skip area in the middle. For a serve or return to be good, it must skip in the designated skip area and pass into the opponent's court. Point systems are worked out for missed catches and bad throws.

**A world-record-breaking tunnel.**

## BACK OFF

Two players start at a very short distance apart (10-15m.). They throw back and forth. Each time a catch is made, they take a step back. First thrower to make the catcher move the pivot foot to catch loses that round. This is sometimes played with two catchers who have one's right leg tied to the other's left. Or it can be played cooperatively with partners trying for maximum number of completions.

## KOSMIC KATASTROPHIES

Few people can play this one because it requires being able to padiddle a disc in each hand at the same time. Two players confront each other gladiator style in a six-foot square court, each with two padiddles going. Players attempt to dislodge the other's padiddles with their own (no body contact allowed). When one player has dropped both discs, play stops and the other player gets a point for each padiddle still going.

## DISCROQUET

This is played just like croquet, except: Hula Hoops serve as wickets, and "sending" is done by throwing both discs at once.

## MANHUNT

This is the usual freeform game except that capture is made by hitting opposing players with a Frisbee disc (below the knees if hard throws are allowed). Lots of players and good terrain are the keys to quality play.

## BUTTERFLY GUTS

This is a great indoor version of Guts and one that is very challenging. Teams of one to five players stand about fifteen feet apart and play Guts as usual except that only butterfly throws may be used.

## TWOBEE

A number of games have been devised around throwing two discs at once. It's necessary to use different sized discs so that one fits inside the other. In one version, two points are scored for catching both discs and none for only one disc unless the catcher can use that disc to hit the second disc while it is still moving, which scores one. No discs caught scores one point for the thrower, and a bad throw scores one for the catcher.

## MOBILE PLAY

Games can be invented for any sort of vehicle play: bicycles, roller skates, skateboards, ice skates, horses, motorcycles, snow skis, and others have all been tried. The simple thrill of catching and throwing on the move is enough at first, but, once you become good on your chosen vehicle, you'll want to come up with a game. Throw, Pedal & Catch is one game.

## CONVERSION

This game, one of the best ever devised for the disc, was developed by Steve Gottlieb and Roger Barrett. It would probably be a major tournament sport except for the fact that it requires a football goal post with plenty of playing room on each side. The two opposing players have a starting line twenty to forty yards on each side of the goal posts (starting lines can be adjusted as handicaps). Players take turns throwing, and the throw must pass through the uprights and over the crossbar to count. A point is lost if a good throw is not caught or if a bad throw is made.

The strategy involves staying on the offensive with long or curving throws that give the opponent little margin for a killer return. Once a player gets backed up or pushed off to one side or in any other no-win situation, he or she may elect to give up a point and the serve to return play to the starting lines.

## MAXI-OP

How many players can play with one throw? One player throws. The receiving players must each control the disc then stand to one side. No score is recorded unless the termination is a trick catch.

## DISC WARS

This involves two teams with lots of players each and three or more discs per player. Each team has a target perched up on a pole as their command post. A ring is drawn around it which no players may enter. The object is to topple the opposing team's target with a throw of the disc. This can be combined with Manhunt, so that opposing player can be captured. Strategy involves capturing discs and getting them to the front lines of the battlefield.

# Appendix II
# World Records

## WORLD RECORDS

OUTDOOR DISTANCE
444 ft. (135.3 m)
John Kirkland, Del Mar CA
April 30, 1978 Dallas TX

INDOOR DISTANCE
296.3 ft. (90.3 m)
Joseph Youngman, L'Anse MI
August 22, 1978 Los Angeles CA

MAXIMUM TIME ALOFT
15.0 seconds
Ken Westerfield, Toronto, Ontario Canada
August, 1975 and
Cliff Towne, Santa Barbara CA
March 26, 1977 Santa Barbara CA

THROW, RUN, AND CATCH
247.5 ft. (75.4 m)
Joseph Youngman, Jackson MI
August 25, 1977 Los Angeles CA

ACCURACY
21 of 28
Tom Kennedy, Santa Barbara CA
August 27, 1977 Los Angeles CA

## WOMEN'S WORLD RECORDS

OUTDOOR DISTANCE
283.5 ft. (86.4 m)
Susane Lempert, New York NY
July 24, 1976 Boston MA

INDOOR DISTANCE
222.5 ft. (67.8 m)
Monika Lou, Boulder CO
August 24, 1977 Los Angeles CA

MAXIMUM TIME ALOFT
9.9 seconds
Monika Lou, Boulder CO
August 27, 1977 Los Angeles CA

9.92 seconds (electronic watch)
Cynthia Allen, Huntsville AL
June 17, 1978 Perryville KY

THROW, RUN, AND CATCH
152.5 ft. (46.9 m)
Teresa Gaman, Palo Alto CA
June 25, 1977 Vancouver, BC Canada

ACCURACY
15 of 28
Monika Lou, Boulder CO
June 12, 1976 Florence AL and
Michele Marini, Albany NY
July 24, 1977 Minneapolis MN

## SENIORS' WORLD RECORDS

OUTDOOR DISTANCE
288 ft. (87.8 m)
Roy Pledger, Austin TX
April 30, 1978 Dallas TX

INDOOR DISTANCE
209.8 ft. (64 m)
Roy Pledger, Austin TX
August 22, 1978 Los Angeles CA

MAXIMUM TIME ALOFT
9.5 seconds
Ralph Williamson, Seattle WA
September 10, 1977 Seattle WA

THROW, RUN, AND CATCH
116 ft. (35.4 m)
Ralph Williamson, Seattle WA
March 26, 1976 Santa Barbara CA

ACCURACY
15 of 28
Jack Roddick, Shippensburg PA
June 25, 1977 New York NY

## JUNIORS' WORLD RECORDS
(16 yrs. and under)

OUTDOOR DISTANCE
388.5 ft. (118.4 m)
Scott Zimmerman, Marietta GA
April 8, 1978 Fredericksburg VA

MAXIMUM TIME ALOFT
10.8 seconds
Krae VanSickle, New York NY
August 7, 1976 Toronto, Ontario

THROW, RUN AND CATCH
169 ft. (51.5 m)
Krae VanSickle, New York NY
August 7, 1976 Toronto, Ontario

ACCURACY
17 of 28
Bruce Tashoff, New York NY
June 25, 1976 New York NY

## CHILDREN'S WORLD RECORDS
(12 years and under)

### OUTDOOR DISTANCE
216 ft. (65.8 m)
Scott McGlasson, Monrovia CA
March 26, 1977 Santa Barbara CA

### MAXIMUM TIME ALOFT
7.9 seconds
Bobby Stanislaus, Monrovia CA
March 26, 1976 Santa Barbara CA

### THROW, RUN, AND CATCH
105 ft. (32 m)
Scott McGlasson, Monrovia CA
March 26, 1976 Santa Barbara CA

### ACCURACY
6 of 28
Bobby Stanislaus, Monrovia CA
April 23, 1977 Irvine CA

(9 yrs. and under)

### OUTDOOR DISTANCE
148 ft. (45.1 m)
Sandy Frentz, Davis CA
May 13, 1978 Sonoma CA

### CANINE DISTANCE
334.6 ft. (102 m)
Dave Johnson throwing for
Martha Faye, Fredericksburg VA
June 11, 1978 Wilmette IL

### 24 HOUR PAIR DISTANCE
323.44 miles (520.53 km)
Brice Gray, Eric Girty, Cincinnati OH
July 21-22, 1977 Cincinnati OH

### MINI DISTANCE
215 ft. (65.5 m)
Craig Mauck, Harrisburg VA
August 25, 1978 Los Angeles CA

## OTHER WORLD RECORDS

### FIELD GOAL
300 ft. (91.4 m)
John Kirkland, Del Mar CA
August 3, 1975 La Canada CA

### GROUP MARATHON
1001 hours
Alhambra Frisbee disc Club
May 7-June 18, 1978 Alhambra CA

### MINI MAXIMUM TIME ALOFT
8.8 seconds
Michael Young, Modesto CA
May 15, 1977 San Francisco CA

### GROUP DISTANCE (24 hour time period)
428.02 miles (688.84 km)
South Windsor Ultimate Frisbee disc Team
July 8-9, 1977 Vernon CT

### MARATHON ULTIMATE
15 hours
Michigan State vs. Kalamazoo College
January, 1975 Kalamazoo MI

### TWO PERSON MARATHON
100 hours
John Kimball and David Goldstein
San Francisco CA
February 15th-19th, 1978

### NAIL DELAY (SELF-THROWN)
43.3 seconds
Marty Johnson, Brier WA
May 14, 1977 San Francisco CA

### ALTITUDE
24,590 ft. (7,495 m)
Christopher Pizzo, Denver CO
August 10, 1977 Pik Kommunizma, USSR

### WHEELCHAIR DISTANCE
149 ft. (45.4 m)
Jay Rohleder, Tempe AZ
May 6, 1978 Tempe AZ

### WHEELCHAIR ACCURACY
9 of 28
Jay Rohleder, Tempe AZ
May 6, 1978 Tempe AZ

## TEAM CHAMPIONSHIPS
### GUTS

| | |
|---|---|
| 1958-1966 | North Central |
| 1967 | Foul Five |
| 1968 | California Masters |
| 1969 | California Masters |
| 1970 | Foul Five |
| 1971 | Highland Avenue Aces |
| 1972 | Highland Avenue Aces |
| 1973 | Highland Avenue Aces |
| 1974 | Library Bar |
| 1975 | Air Aces |
| 1976 | Air Aces |
| 1977 | Library Bar |
| 1978 | Library Bar |

### ULTIMATE

| | |
|---|---|
| 1973 | Rutgers University |
| 1974 | Rutgers University |
| 1975 | Rutgers University |
| 1976 | Rutgers University |
| 1977 | Santa Barbara |
| 1978 | Santa Barbara |

### DYNAMO DISC

| | |
|---|---|
| 1976 | Berkeley Flashers |
| 1977 | Oakland Streakers |
| 1978 | Hayward Flashers |

# Glossary

**Accelerations**-Any discwork technique used to add spin to the disc, particularly brushes, twirls, and padiddles.

**Ace**-A Guts throw that passes through the receiving line untouched.

**Aids**-Devices such as thimbles, sticks, and flying disc rings used in freestyle to control the disc.

**Air bounce**-A style of throwing in which the disc is forced to rebound off a cushion of air that piles up under its belly.

**Approach shot**-In golf, any throw with the aim of gaining putting position.

**Arch line**-In Dynamo Disc, the semicircle around each goal that can be entered only by one offensive and one defensive player.

**Attitude**-The angle of the disc with reference to the shoulder axis. Nose up is called positive attitude. Nose down is called negative attitude.

**Attitude reversal**-Any change in the disc's attitude in flight, especially from negative to positive.

**Backhand**-A cross-body throw with the thumb on top of the disc and the fingers under it.

**Backslide**-A freestyle move in which a dead disc is made to slide down the back.

**Bank**-A curve steep enough to have a pronounced peak.

**Barrel roll**-Exaggerated turnover in flight.

**Basket**-In golf, a container-type target on the ground.

**Belly**-The concave side of the disc.

**Berkeley grip**-A backhand grip with the forefinger hooked around the rim and the other fingers curled back to or nearly to the cheek.

**Blind**-Any catch or throw performed while looking away from the disc or the target.

**Bobble**-1. A missed catching attempt followed by repeated efforts to make a catch before the disc hits the ground. 2. In Guts, batting the disc gently upward until the top thrower can make the catch.

**Body rolls**-Any freestyle move in which a portion of the body is used as a surface for the disc to roll on.

**Body skips**-Any freestyle move in which the skip edge of the disc is allowed to strike the player to produce a skip.

**Bomb**-A long downfield pass in Ultimate.

**Bottom**-The belly of the disc.

**Break tip**-The initial contact made with a disc in flight to alter the attitude and speed for further discwork.

**Brush**-Any propulsion or acceleration of the disc from a glancing slap on the lip.

**Btb**-Behind the back.

**Bth**-Behind the head.

**Btl**-Between the legs.

**Burbled air**-Turbulent, unpredictable wind.

**Burn**-A low, flat, speedy throw in Double Disc Court.

**Butterfly**-1. The motion of a disc flipping end over end. 2. A throw made by flipping the disc end over end.

**Catapult**-Any of a variety of throws launched by a flip of the finger.

**Center**-To pass the disc toward the center of the field in Ultimate.

**Check**-After a foul or a traveling call in Ultimate, the defensive player guarding the passer holds the disc until play is ready to resume.

**Cheek**-The inside rim of the disc.

**Chop**-The sharpest possible brush, adding spin but little or no propulsion. Also known as a thumb brush or knock-down brush.

**Clear and fill**-An Ultimate tactic in which the offense spreads out to open a space downfield for a player to streak through and receive a pass.

**Clock spin**-The spin imparted by a right-handed backhand or staker or a left handed sidearm or wrist flip.

**Closed stance**-The throwing position for backhands and stakers.

**Constorksion**-Any termination made in a contorted position, named for the originator, Dan "Stork" Roddick.

**Continuations**-Any discwork technique used to control the flight of the disc, particularly delays, tips, and MACs (Includes accelerations and maintenance).

**Co-oping**-Discwork shared by two or more players.

**Counterbrush**-A brush made in the opposite direction from the spin on the disc.

**Counterspin**-The spin imparted by a left-handed backhand or staker or a right-handed sidearm or wrist flip.

**Crescent roll**-A roller that lands at a very shallow angle so that it curves sharply off at a right angle to the line of flight.

**Cross-body**-Any catch or throw made with the arm reaching across the chest.

**Crown**-The top of the disc.

**Cuff**-Holding the disc with the nonthrowing hand before or during the stroke.

**Curve roller**-A roller thrown to land roughly straight up so that it will curve off to the backside.

**Delay**-To control a spinning disc by continuous contact with the flight plate.

**Delivery**-The entire throwing motion.

**Deflection**-Any change in the course of the disc's flight caused by contact with the lip.

**Dip**-Any sudden drop during a disc's flight, particularly when the disc rises afterward.

**Directional**-An intentional deflection.

**Disc Pole Hole**-A standardized golf target devised by Ed Headrick.

**Discwork**-Any move used to control a disc.

**Dishing**-The helixing motion of a disc sliding with only one point on the edge touching the ground.

**Double**-In DDC, when both discs are touched simultaneously by the members of one team.

**Drop**-1. A missed catch that falls to the ground. 2. The descent of the disc, particularly the level descent as part of a freestyle move.

**Edge**-The bottommost portion of the rim.

**Facing stance**-A throwing position in which the thrower faces directly toward the target.

**Fan grip**-A backhand grip with the forefinger along the rim and the other fingers spread out on the flight plate.

**Finger flip**-A catapult in which the disc is held by one launching finger and one cuffing finger.

**Flamingo**-A btl catch made near the ground while on one leg, usually of a drop.

**Flamingitis**-A flamingo made by reaching back through the legs.

**Flight axis**-An imaginary line through the center of a flying disc from nose to tail.

**Flight plate**-Formerly, the top surface of the disc, but generally now the plate from rim to rim, both top and bottom.

**Flight rings**-Concentric rings on the flight plate of Wham-O discs.

**Flip-out**-A technique for setting a disc up by hooking the fingers in the cheek and twisting the forearm.

**Floater**-A hover.

**Flow**-A subcategory of Presentation in freestyle judging—a subjective estimation of the degree to which a routine hangs together.

**Fluff**-Using one or both forearms to control the disc by making contact with the edges (right side up) or the flight plate (upside-down).

**Folf**-An early name for disc golf.

**Forgivingness**-The extent to which bad throws go unpunished on a golf course.

**Freeze**-Any trap of the disc made by pressing against the lip.

**Give and go**-A passing technique in Ultimate in which one player, after completing a short pass, sprints to collect a return pass.

**Glide phase**-The most nearly level portion in the descent of a throw, particularly in MTA, TRC, and Distance.

**Groove**-The particular throwing motion that yields the most power the most efficiently and that can be duplicated on repeated attempts.

**Guide**-Any freestyle move in which the disc is propelled by continuous light pressure against the lip.

**Gym-floor curve**-A throwing technique in which the disc is made to skim over the ground standing on its skip shoulder.

**Gyre**-A slight wobbling motion seen in a spinning disc that is unbalanced or warped.

**Helix**-The wobbling or rocking motion sometimes seen in a slowly spinning or dead disc that is subjected to uneven forces.

**Hesitation**-1. Any move in which the disc is controlled by light contact against the lip, including guides. 2. A balk in a freestyle routine.

**Hook thumber**-A cross-body throw with the thumb against the cheek and the fingers on top of the disc.

**Hoop**-The Accuracy target.

**Hover**-A type of flight in which the disc has little or no forward momentum and descends slowly.

**Hyperspin**-Extreme rotation.

**Hyzer**-1. The tendency of a disc to rotate around its flight axis. (Most discs lift slightly at the roll shoulder.) 2. The degree to which this tendency must be compensated for in the angle of release to produce the desired flight angle.

**It's up**-A call in Ultimate to alert teammates that the disc has been thrown.

**Inflection points**-Slight hops or attitude reversals in the flight of a disc, particularly in the glide phase.

**Intolerable delay**-A delay that continues until the spin is exhausted.

**Killer pass**-In Ultimate, a pass that penetrates deep into the defense.

**Lead**-To throw ahead of a receiver so that a pass can be caught in stride.

**Left curve**-A term that has been used for both a throw to the left that curves to the right and a throw to the right that curves to the left.

**Left spin**-A term that has been used to mean both clock spin and counterspin.

**Lie**-1. The point at which a disc comes to rest in golf. 2. What golf players usually do about their score.

**Lip**-The outside rim of a disc.

**Luft**-A full-handed tip.

**MAC**-Midair attitude control. Any techniques for changing the attitude of a disc, particularly a top tip on the roll shoulder.

**Maintenance**-Any continuation technique which does not add to the spin of the disc.

**Micronesia**-Freestyle played at very close range.

**Milking**-Waiting until the last possible moment to make a catch, especially in MTA and DDC.

**Move**-Any act of throwing, controlling, or catching a disc, often used to refer to a series of disc-work tricks as well.

**Multiple skips**-Steep skip flights that result in two or more skips.

**Native spin**-The spin imparted by the original propulsion before any acceleration moves.

**Necrophilia**-Any moves performed with a nonspinning disc. Also known as deadwork.

**Normal curve**-A term sometimes used for a skip curve.

**Normal spin**-A term sometimes used for clock spin.

**Nose**-The leading edge of a disc in flight.

**Nose gliding**-Wind-propelled, negative-attitude flight.

**Open stance**-The throwing position for forehand and overhand throws.

**Optimum effort**-In Guts, to rise to full height and extend an arm upward to full length—the minimum necessary effort for determining if a high or wide throw was out of reach.

**Padiddle**-Spinning the disc with circular motion of the finger on the flight plate.

**Pancake**-1. Trapping the disc between both hands. Also called a sandwich trap. 2. The flattening out motion of an upside-down lob throw.

**Pick-up**-Any technique used to retrieve a disc from the ground.

**Platforming**-An extended attitude reversal so that the disc travels a good distance nearly horizontal.

**Precession**-The motion of a spinning disc when a torque (off-center force) is applied.

**Propulsions**-Any technique used to impart spin to a disc.

**Puddle catch**-An upside-down finger-spinning catch.

**Pull**-1. The throw-off in Ultimate. 2. Backhand throws from a facing stance.

**Push**-1. A guide. 2. Any throw made with the hand on the tail of the disc.

**Question-mark curve**-A hook-thumber gym-floor curve.

**Reach**-The distance from the axis of body rotation to the center of the disc for distance throws. For example, a sidearm has a longer reach than a backhand because the disc is gripped further out in the hand and because the body can be more off-center during delivery.

**Reverse curve**-A term sometimes used for roll curves.

**Reverse spin**-A term sometimes used for counter spin.

**Ridge work**-Delay moves employing the flight rings, particularly the inner rings of a Super-Pro.

**Right curve**-A term that has been used for both a throw to the left that curves to the right and a throw to the right that curves to the left.

**Right spin**-A term that has been used to mean both clock spin and counter spin.

**Rim**-The hoop portion of a disc—the lip, cheek, and edge.

**Rim delay**-A delay in which the contact is against the cheek.

**Roll curve**-A curved flight in which the roll shoulder is lower so that the disc tends to roll when it lands.

**Roll shoulder**-The shoulder of the disc that spins back toward the thrower.

**Scoop**-A deadwork technique in which the disc is maneuvered by continuous pressure on the flight plate.

**Scrambling**-Chasing after a deflected disc in Guts.

**Set-up**-1. Any method of imparting spin to a disc without propulsion. 2. To get in position for a particular move.

**Shade**-To guard a passer more to one side than another.

**Shelf**-The point in an MTA throw when the disc stalls in a level attitude.

**Shoulder axis**-An imaginary line through the center of a flying disc from roll shoulder to skip shoulder.

**Shoulders**-The sides of a disc in flight, ninety degrees from the nose or tail.

**Siamese catch**-Any simultaneous catch by two or more players.

**Sidearm**-A forehand throw made with the middle finger (usually) against the cheek and the thumb on top of the disc.

**Skip curve**-A curved flight in which the skip shoulder is lower so that the disc tends to skip when it lands.

**Skip shoulder**-The shoulder of the disc that spins away from the thrower.

**Slider**-A disc moving with the edge flat on the ground.

**Spin axis**-An imaginary line through the center of the disc perpendicular to the flight plate.

**Spinner**-A throw released from twirling on the finger.

**Spin-off**-A throw made from a freeze position.

**Sprue**-The slight bump in the center of a disc left from the injection of the plastic into the mold.
**Stability**-The property of a disc to maintain flight at the angle of release—the ability to resist turnover.
**Staker**-The hook-thumb throw.
**Stall**-That portion of some flights at which the disc loses forward momentum.
**Stalling**-A defensive call in Ultimate when the passer is taking too much time, followed by a countdown.
**Stroke**-1. Any throw in golf. 2. The forward-moving portion of the delivery.
**Sweep**-A trailing-edge catch with the arm extended at shoulder height.
**Tacking**-When a disc holds its course across a wind.
**Tail**-The rear end of a disc in flight.
**Tailskate**-Extreme positive-attitude flight in a heavy tailwind.
**Terminations**-Any move which arrests the flight or spin of a disc, particularly catches, traps, and drops.
**Throw-off**-1. The long pass to the opposing team that begins play in Ultimate. 2. The exchange of passes that begins play in DDC.
**Thumber**-A forehand throw made with the thumb against the cheek and the fingers curled over the lip.
**Tipping**-Control of a disc by percussive contact with the flight plate.
**Top**-The convex side of the disc—the crown.
**Top work**-Discwork in which contact is made on the top of a rightside-up disc. Also known as topping.
**Touch**-Appropriate speed and spin in putting.
**Tower**-The portion of an MTA flight that sometimes occurs after the shelf in which the disc lifts straight upward several feet.
**Trail**-Any catch made by grasping the disc by the tail as it passes.
**Trap**-A type of catch in which the disc is stopped between any two parts of the body or even a part of the body and another surface.
**Tricking**-Performing discwork techniques.
**Tunnel**-A noncontact discwork technique in which the disc is allowed to pass through a hoop formed by a player's limbs.
**Turnover**-1. The tendency of a flying disc to rotate about the flight axis. 2. A discwork technique in which the disc is turned from upside-down to rightside-up or vice versa.
**Underhand**-A noncross-body backhand throw.
**Veer roller**-A roller thrown to land at a sharp angle so that it angles off to the inside.
**Wrist flip**-An overhand throw made with the thumb on the belly and the fingers fanned out on top.
**Zeno point**-The point in the descent of a dropping disc or one rolling or dishing on the ground at which it is perfectly aligned for a brush.
**Zeno throw**-A hyperspin underhand throw.
**Z's**-Spin.

# Acknowledgments

Sam Barron contributed an exceptional amount of work in putting this book together, and the authors wish to thank him for his help.

Many Frisbee disc players have provided the authors with advice and comments over the years, much of which is reflected in this text. Jo Cahow and the staff at the International Frisbee disc Association provided able assistance.

Many thanks also to Lynne Steele, Joe Davis, Steve Gottlieb, Tom McRann, Dudley and Teresa, Walter Wright, Carol Nathan, John Connelly, Doug Newland, Dan Poynter, Dave Zouzounis and the Flying Disc Artists, and E. Tallulah de Fort Worth.

A special thanks to Jack Roddick for giving Stork his first disc.

PHOTOGRAPH IDENTIFICATION KEY

Page 1—Laura Engel; p. 3—Krae VanSickle; p. 5—Shayna Gaman; p. 6—Peter Bloeme & Châu Rottman; p. 7—Junichi Kumakura; p. 12—Gee Kirkland; p. 14—Erwin Velasquez & Jens Velasquez.

Chapter 1: p. 15—Bob Ennis; pp. 16-17—John Kirkland; p. 20—Ken Westerfield, Tom Monroe; p. 21—Cynthia Allen; p. 23—Tom McRann; p. 26—Charles Tips; p. 27—Teresa Gaman.

Chapter 2: p. 29—Tom McRann, Joe Youngman, Teresa Gaman; p. 32—Tom McRann; p. 33—Buzz Laughlin.

Chapter 3: p. 34—Terrie Houle & Marie Bracciale; p. 35—Jim Palmeri & John Kirkland: p. 36—Alan Fridge & Laura Engel, Terrence Tips, Dan Roddick & John Kirkland, Jonathon Hatfield; p. 37—Dan Roddick, Tom Monroe; p. 40—Dan Roddick & John Kirkland, Jonathon Hatfield; p. 41—Jeff Burke, Dan Roddick.

Chapter 4: p. 42—Mark Horn; p. 43— Roy Pledger, Mike Conger; p. 44—Jeff Burke; p. 45—John Connelly; p. 46—Jeff Soto; p. 49—Jeff Soto; p. 50—Agneta Fuglesang, Cynthia Allen, Jeff Burke, Carolyn McRorie; p. 52—Victor Malafronte, Jeff Soto.

Chapter 5: p. 52—Peter Bloeme; p. 53—Jim Brown, John Weyand, Moises Alfaro; p. 54—Jens Velasquez; p. 55—Teresa Gaman, Evan David; p. 56—Paul Hooston, Peter Bloeme, John Kirkland; p. 57—John Anthony, Paul Thompson; p. 59—Dave Marini (bottom), Sammy Schatz; p. 60—Kevin Aiello, Don Hoskins, Randy Osborne; p. 61—John Kirkland; p. 62—John Kirkland, Don Hoskins; p. 63—Kevin Givens, Don Hoskins; p. 64—John Dwork, Jo Cahow; p. 65—Tom Wingo; p. 66—Tony Zweig (bottom), Kevin Sullivan (r); p. 67—George Morris (top 1), Maryann Bowman (bottom); p. 68—Corey Basso; p. 70—Krae VanSickle, John Kirkland & Bill King, Freddie Haft & Dan Roddick, Moises Alfaro & Danny McInnis, Brian Roberts & John Jewell; p. 71—Peter Bloeme & Châu Rottman, Bill King & John Kirkland; p. 72—Bob Ennis & Danny McInnis, Evan David & Corey Basso, John Jewell, Matt Roberts & Brian Roberts; pp. 72-73—Steve Gottlieb, John Jewell & Hal Ericson; p. 74-Kai Bune, Marty Johnson, Jeff Elliot & Doug Newland; p. 75—Dan Roddick & Freddie Haft, Michelle Pezzoli & Cyndi Birch.

Chapter 6: p. 76—Châu Rottman & Randy Osborne; p. 77—Charles Duval, Harold Duval, Irv Kalb, Tim Selinske & Tom Ross, Charles Duval; p. 80—Irv Kalb, Tim Selinske, Joe Youngman & Châu Rottman; p. 81— Steve McLean; p. 84—Tim Selinske, Alan Bonopane (top r), Joe Youngman, Châu Rottman, Randy Osborne, John Connelly; p. 85—Ray Mueller & Mike Young, José Montalvo, Steve Matul & David Bradshaw; p. 87—Ray Mueller, Mike Young & Charles Tips.

Chapter 7: p. 89—Doug Newland, Tom Kennedy, George Morris; p. 91—Gerry Geare & Peter Bloeme, Jon Cohn & Charles Duval; p. 92—Dave Zouzounis, Tony Zweig, Peter Martin & Robin Melanson, Peter Bloeme, John Weyand & Jeff Jorgenson; p. 93— Tom Kennedy & Jim Herrick, Peter Martin & Ray Mueller; p. 97— Victor Malafronte & Walter White, Ray Mueller; p. 98—Don Cain, Jim Herrick & Tom Kennedy; p. 99—Tom Monroe, Gerry Geare, Châu Rottman, Jeff Jorgenson, Jens Velasquez; p. 104— Charlie Mensinger; p. 107—John Pickerill & Martha; p. 119—Jens Velasquez; p. 120 Jack Roddick.